WHAT IS AN EMPATH?

A Beginner's Guide to Understanding Empaths

Josie Barrett

© Copyright 2021 - All rights reserved.

The content contained within this book may not be reproduced, duplicated or transmitted without direct written permission from the author or the publisher, Josie Barrett. For requests, please email Josie at jb@josiebarrett.com.

Under no circumstances will any blame or legal responsibility be held against the publisher, or author, for any damages, reparation, or monetary loss due to the information contained within this book, either directly or indirectly.

Legal Notice:

This book is copyright protected. It is only for personal use. You cannot amend, distribute, sell, use, quote or paraphrase any part, or the content within this book, without the consent of the author or publisher.

Disclaimer Notice:

Please note the information contained within this document is for educational and entertainment purposes only. All effort has been executed to present accurate, up to date, reliable, complete information. No warranties of any kind are declared or implied. Readers acknowledge that the author is not engaged in the rendering of legal, financial, medical or professional advice. The content within this book has been derived from various sources. Please consult a licensed professional before attempting any techniques outlined in this book.

By reading this document, the reader agrees that under no circumstances is the author responsible for any losses, direct or indirect, that are incurred as a result of the use of the information contained within this document, including, but not limited to, errors, omissions, or inaccuracies.

Table of Contents

Table of Contents 3
Author's Note to Reader 6
Introduction 7
Chapter 1: Defining the Empath and Empathy 12
    The Highly Sensitive Person and the Empath 16
    Types of Empaths 19
        Emotional Empaths 21
        Physical and Medical Empaths 23
        Claircognizant and Intuitive Empaths 26
        Earth and Geomantic Empaths................................. 28
        Fauna and Animal Empaths 31
        Psychic and Medium Empaths 33
        Psychometric Empaths 36
        Precognitive Empaths 38
        Telepathic Empaths 40
        Heyoka—Sacred Clown Empath 41
        Dream Empaths 45
    The Myers-Briggs Connection 46

Affective, Somatic, and Cognitive Empathy 49

Chapter 2: Solid Signs That You Are an Empath 52

Can You Relate? 53

Positive and Negative Aspects of Being an Empath 63

Positive Aspects 65

Negative Aspects 69

A Discussion on the Aspects of Being an Empath 72

Chapter 3: Scientific Theories of Empathic Abilities 75

The Mirror Neuron System 76

Emotional Contagion 79

Electromagnetic Fields 80

Synesthesia 82

Chapter 4: The Spiritual Theory—Energy and Psychics in the New Age 84

The Saboteur 86

The Victim 88

The Prostitute 89

The Child 90

Spiritual Gifts and Psychic Intuition 92

Chapter 5: Religion and the Empath 96

Chapter 6: Empaths and the Law of Attraction 99

What Is the Law of Attraction? 100

A Guide for the Empath on the Law of Attraction 102

    Finding the Core Self..104

    Balancing the Heart and Mind to Work as One 105

    Live the Life of Choice...107

Chapter 7: The Connection Between Empaths and Narcissism 109

    What Is the Dark Empath and Why Do Psychologists Fear Them? 111

    Recognizing the Warning Signs 112

Chapter 8: Is it Mine or Someone Else's?............................... 115

Chapter 9: Tools and Suggestions for the Empath................ 118

    Meditation, Awareness, and Being Present 118

    Holding Supportive Space..120

    The Empath in the Workplace..122

        Careers that Work 122

        Careers That Do Not Seem to Work....................... 123

Conclusion..124

Acknowledgments.. 127

About the Author 129

References 131

Image References 137

Author's Note to Reader

Dear Reader,

This book contains a great deal of information. Some of that information is more difficult to digest than others, especially the chapters dealing with scientific theories. I realize this and encourage you to read the parts that you are drawn to first. The book is a guide, designed for you to be able to skip chapters and come back to them when you are ready. Take time to digest the information and don't worry about rushing through reading the whole book. This was all the information that I sought in my own journey of discovering the empath. I wanted all of that information to be organized for you sensibly, but that doesn't mean I came upon it all in such an organized way. So go ahead and read what you want first. In addition, I called this a beginner's guide because it is meant to begin you on your own journey of discovery. All of my references are in the back of the book. I encourage you to use these to dig deeper into the areas that interest you. Let your unique journey begin...

With appreciation,

Josie

Introduction

Christian Keyser, neuroscientist and author of *The Empathic Brain: How the Discovery of Mirror Neurons Changes Our Understanding of Human Nature,* speaks about empathy. He states that decades ago we thought that we only activated our visual cortex when witnessing something happening to another person. We now know that we activate our own actions, emotions, and sensations as if we would feel the same in that situation (Armstrong, 2017).

When you were little, you most likely went through a phase where you would mimic the adults around you. You also wanted to be just like an adult and played adult-like games. This phase in a child's life is imperative to them learning the theory of mind later on (Ruhl, 2020). Theory of mind is the ability to attribute mental states to the people around us and to ourselves. Not all people have a strong theory of mind and individuals who have low levels of theory of mind may possess levels of schizophrenia, social anxiety, depression, or autism or Asperger's Syndrome.

Empaths have a heightened theory of mind. They also intrigue the world of psychology and are at the forefront of many studies (Decety, 2010). While the nature, reason, and core aspects of empathy are being furiously studied to be understood, empaths themselves have really been left in the dark. The empathic nature is the golden lab rat of the 21st century, and empaths are the pseudoscience hiding under the stairs and anxiously waiting for some validation of their mere existence.

Are empaths a myth? No. Are empaths pseudoscience? Yes and no. Yes to the world of science, because empaths are so vastly different that they cannot be bagged, tagged, and sold in pill form for a profit and so they are thrown into the same pocket as quantum subjects, ghosts, and bending spoons. Scientists measure a thousand things against the speed of light, which has never been measured, and that is why they use Einstein's theory of relativity (*The One-Way Speed of Light | Spaceaustralia*, 2021). Yesterday string theory was thrown out the window after being called a "broken box of dreams," and yet when the theory itself gave the world it's structured beauty it was the law taught and debated by all and rejected by none (Siegel, 2021).

What we do know for certain is that empathy exists, and there are people who are genetically inclined to be naturally more empathic than others (Riess, 2017). Is there a way to become an empath if your brain is not wired in such a way naturally? This we do not have an answer for. We do know that empathy is needed, and if it were possible that we could create a world of "empathically inclined" people, then the world would be a better place for all. While science leans toward the empaths' favor but does not give it any, and the spiritual New Age world leans a little too far into providing the empathic person a superhero's personality, we need to keep our wits about us and really understand what the empath is.

I do not promise you that you are a superhero or that you will be able to mimic the feelings of every person and remove sickness from the dying. However, I do promise you that by the end of this book you will have better direction into who and what an empath is and why they are different from a highly sensitive individual. I also promise you that you will be able to navigate your inner landscape far better and will have the hope of replacing your fears.

I promise that the information that I will give to you within this book will empower you as a person, regardless of the type of empath that you are. You will find your direction, and you will be empowered with facts within the scientific and spiritual realms without being forced into any belief system. It is my wish that you find your own path and understand that no one can ever dictate to you about who you are and who you are not. Only you have the power to understand yourself, and there is nothing on this planet that knows you better than you know yourself.

It is my opinion that each and every person simply needs unbiased information to be able to successfully navigate this life. With this unbiased information, we have the freedom to be able to make up our own minds and therefore lead our own lives. When we follow someone else's opinions blindly without being given the liberty to make up our own minds, we will never be steered down the right path.

Within this book, you will find guidance, expert research, and the opinions of both sides of the world of science as well as various spiritual contexts. You will also be given the universal picture of what an empath is and what empathy is and how to use it effectively. You will become able to understand yourself and other empaths who may be different from you. With all of this information, it is my hope that you will find a deep sense of inner peace and purpose to use what you were born with to assist the rest of the world in becoming a better place.

There are many books on the market that promise the empath and those who live with an empath, concrete answers. Some of them offer fantastic advice for empaths, but most of these books are concentrated on the view of the author, which is not a holistic one. What you need is a holistic picture of the entire spectrum of information regardless of my opinion. Of course, my own beliefs may shine through in the sentences, and this cannot be avoided unless I write an academic paper on the subject. What you do get from me is a holistic picture and a world map that encompasses the spiritual, the scientific, and the cultural aspects in the pseudoscience of the world of empaths and empathy.

I will also present to you the darkness that lies within the potential of all empaths and those who have more in their personality bucket and who are, in fact, a danger within society—the dark empaths.

I will show you the difference between being an empath and having empathy, the possibility of being a highly sensitive individual, and being an empath on the wrong side of the tracks. I will provide you with the foundational means to be able to understand your place within the empathic realm of existence and do it in such a way that you will be able to pick and choose what resonates with you and what doesn't.

Always remember to take only that which resonates with you. Remember that the world is still young, and despite the fact that the era of information is upon us, we have much to learn, much to understand, and even more to experience. You are your own worst enemy and your own best friend. Make sure that you are rooting for yourself, and that you always follow your inner voice. Nothing anyone says is the law. What you say over your own life is.

Chapter 1: Defining the Empath and Empathy

In the world of psychology, it has been found that empathy development is genetic. Development in a child is attributed to the care received from the mother more than the father (American Psychological Association, 2019). We also have evidence that proto-empathic abilities have been found in apes and possibly in monkeys. The studies in the science world are really all over the place, from studying how our genetics influence our sense of compassion and theory of mind, to the similarity between empathy in humans and those in animals. There is no evidence as of yet to prove that non-human apes have empathic abilities, and so we cannot assume that empathy is only reserved for the human gene.

Human empathy is defined as "the ability to detect, predict, or attribute an emotional state of a conspecific, understand the experience of that emotional state, and have an emotional response to the emotional state of the conspecific" (Center for Academic Research & Training in Anthropogeny, n.d.). While this is the generally accepted definition, it is also understood that a lack of empathy in any individual is now understood to be a sure sign of a mental disorder and neurodevelopment pathologies.

Empathy has two extremes, one being simple compassion based on one's own experience, and the other being a physical manifestation that is thought to mirror that of the other person. What separates empathy and the empath is the trigger that sets off the experience (Inge, 2020). The trigger can be anything for someone with a heightened level of empathy. Even the person who experiences physical manifestations that are almost precisely the same as the person who they are feeling empathy toward needs a trigger. This is not the definition of an empath.

While empaths show empathy, they do not need a trigger response to show this empathy, and sometimes they do not even have a conscious idea where the feelings, ideas, and emotions are coming from. Many empaths feel very lost, whereas the person who feels empathy knows exactly why they feel the way they do and does not misunderstand the experience.

An empath who is not consciously shielding their energy and who is perhaps not even aware of the fact that they are an empath may believe that there is something wrong with them. With the influx of many different emotions throughout a single day, becoming worse within crowded areas, an empath may experience mood swings, various physiological changes that come and go all the time, and headaches. Many of these symptoms are commonly mistaken for bipolar disorder and many empaths are wrongly diagnosed as such (Myles, 2017).

People with empathy alone, compared to empaths, are not subjected to a thousand different feelings in a single day. Empathic people know how to differentiate between their feelings and the feelings of the people they are feeling empathy toward. Empathic people are also quite aware of their desire to be compassionate and need to assist. Empaths, on the other hand, may or may not be aware of their desire to assist humanity. The shadow side of an empath who is lost, afraid, and scared to venture into the outside world but does not know why, is someone who no longer wants to help humanity at all. One would never say this about an empath, but as this earth is known to be a world of duality, the empath has a dualistic nature.

The dualistic nature of the human being is sometimes referred to as the shadow side. It is impossible to work through one's shadow and then be done with it. The shadow never leaves and will change over time. Aspects of the shadow self can be healed and transformed to be used within positive traits of character. Shadow work, which is what we call working with our negative or harmful character traits, is not something which we practice, like a sport or a course. Even though many people sell journals, which promise effective shadow side eradication, this is simply marketing and impossible.

Your shadow side will always be with you. In psychology, the hidden aspects of the self are explained through what is known as the "Johari window." This concept is fascinating and comes to prove how our shadow side may become smaller and be immensely healed but it will never disappear. It is better to heal shadow aspects of the self through acknowledgment, authenticity, and hard work. The shadow side is not something to be ashamed of, as it may simply be something that we believe is not considered a social norm.

As you can see, the empath is a channel or conduit for emotions, feelings, thoughts, and experiences, whereas the individual with a high or low sense of empathy will react to certain triggers such as a song. Empathic people can be using their level of ToM, which, even though we discussed this briefly in the introduction, is important enough to explain in detail here.

Uta Frith, a developmental psychologist, reminds us that the only way that we actually found the first idea of the theory of mind is through studying autism and how autistic children develop differently from children who do not have autism. While mentioning her work on the theory of mind, I must also mention her ingenious findings on the difference between empathy and the theory of mind. She speaks about how an empathic person may very well be using the theory of mind to attribute certain behavior and mental workings to another person. Through the use of theory of mind, they are able to 'know' how to assist another person or communicate effectively with them. If people are showing heightened levels of empathy, they are, in fact, using what is known as behavioral contagion (Serious Science, 2016).

Theory of mind can be tested through the Sally-Anne Test, which is one of many used to identify levels of autism. The Sally-Anne Test provides the patient with a story:

> There are two friends, Sally and Anne. Sally has a basket. Anne has a box. Sally has a marble, and she places it in her basket. She then covers her basket and tells her friend that she must go to the bathroom. While she is

gone, Anne is very naughty and takes the marble out of her basket and puts it in her own box. When Sally returns from the bathroom, where will she look for her marble?

If the patient answers the question with "in Anne's box" or another way that refers to the box and not to where Sally last left the marble, the patient is then thought to have little to no theory of mind, and further tests are used to identify the level of theory of mind. The logic in this story for many people would be to place themselves in Sally's shoes. In her shoes, you would have no knowledge of what happened in the room when you were in the bathroom, and so you would imagine that everything was exactly the same as when you left for the bathroom. This would mean that you would return to the last place that you left your marble. To an autistic patient, if they have knowledge of something, then everyone should naturally have that knowledge as well.

Theory of mind is also extremely high in people who lie very well. Lies require great understanding and concentration across all levels of communication to be successful, and someone with a great theory of mind can lie extremely well because they can read the outcome of the other person's acceptance or rejection of the lie that they have been told. It is said that people who are on the autistic spectrum cannot lie.

The Highly Sensitive Person and the Empath

The empath and the highly sensitive person (HSP) are usually mistaken for one another. The truth is that the HSP may very well suffer from what is known as sensory processing sensitivity (SPS) (Goldberg & Scharf, 2020). This sensitivity is not always present in the empath. There are many types of empaths, as we will look at in greater detail in the next section, but there is only one type of HSP. These HSPs are subject to continuous bombardment from the world around them. The empath who happens to be an HSP is bombarded by this sensory overload in addition to being able to pull this overload into themselves, whether they are aware of it or not.

To illustrate the difference, imagine a ball with arrows hitting it. The HSP is this ball and the arrows hitting it on the surface are the sensory overload. This is why HSPs hide away and are always seen as introverts. Now, imagine the ball again. This time the arrows pierce the surface of the ball, and the ball changes color to match that of the arrows. Every arrow changes the ball until, without assistance and survival techniques, the ball begins to think that it is an arrow. This is the empath.

The empath can be an extrovert or an introvert. Regardless of the position that they hold in their interpersonal communication, the difference between the empath and the HSP lies in the empath's ability to absorb everything that it comes into contact with. This absorption is not taking, it is one of two things: either the empath mimics the feelings of the someone or people they come into contact with, or they intuitively manifest similar feelings out of their own.

The HSP is never sitting in the same boat as someone else; they are being bombarded without understanding. Sensory processing sensitivity is non-engaging. The HSP is feeling everything around them, but they are not sharing the experience with the person with whom they come into contact with. The empath is sharing this experience, and all experiences, continuously.

The only similarities are that both the HSP and the empath are capable of feeling deeply, and feeling a sense of being themselves when they find themselves in a place where there is no one or nothing around them. Obviously, a life in a room with no connection to the outside world is not conducive to a healthy mindset at all. For example, the global pandemic allowed people to feel what being cut off from the outside world really feels like, and it transformed so many lives in the process. Unfortunately, so many empaths and HSPs are labeled as being completely anti-social. It is something that cannot be avoided. What if in a quiet space away from the world, the empath and the HSP find themselves? For the HSP, this introverted life becomes second nature, and they are generally far more comfortable with this than the empath who is not naturally an introvert.

The extroverted empaths find themselves fighting the feeling of being left alone and cut off from the world. At exactly the same time, they wish for a space of their own to find solace and breathing space. This continuous war in the mind of the empath keeps them living life with one foot in the world outside and one foot in trying to experience who they really are on a continuous basis. When the world is in crisis, the empath and the HSP both have an incredibly difficult time concentrating on what matters. The HSP is feeling everything and must learn to deal with the emotional overload. The empath needs to deal with this emotional overload and overwhelming sensory input that seems to never end, while also coming in and out of reality.

The HSP can remain aware without any form of external training, whereas the empaths find themselves often thinking why on earth they just made a certain decision, or what plagued their minds for the last half an hour so that they find themselves crying uncontrollably when there is nothing to really cry about? This deep emotion that the empath feels but does not belong to the empath not only manifests in emotional ups and downs, but also has diverse ways of manifesting. Therefore, there are different classifications of empaths.

Types of Empaths

The manner in which each empath absorbs the state of another person and how this state manifests within their being differs from empath to empath. There are no two empaths who are precisely the same, as each one has a little bit of a difference. For example, it is very possible for an emotional empath to be an undercover 'heyoka.' It is probable that an intuitive empath will also have empathic dream states and telepathic abilities that broaden their empathic filters.

It is extremely difficult to categorize empaths because there are so many different nuances in their personalities and the manner in which empaths soak up the world around them. It is also a harrowing task to categorize empaths because the scientific world has not allowed for such a categorization to be captured. It is for this reason that we must look at our own experience as well as the experiences of tens of thousands of empaths who have expressed their own encounters.

Within the detailed accounts from empaths, we find certain patterns begin to emerge. It is in these patterns where we find an understanding, however broad and surface-orientated it seems, that is an understanding, nonetheless. This comprehension allows us to categorize the various types of empaths into their most common forms of existence.

This categorization may not be grounded in science per se, but it is grounded in personal experience and extensive research. If you are an empath, it is not uncommon for you to feel that you share characteristics with more than one type of empath. The intention behind this categorization is not to give the empath another box to be placed in or meaning to something that we have only begun to touch the tip of the iceberg. Instead, this list below is a guide for those who wish to understand the empath, and for the empaths to find guidance and a newfound comprehension around how magically vast their own abilities are. The list is also intended to bring understanding to those who believe that they have lost the plot, are suffering from hallucinations, or have settled in the belief that they are an alien in their own bodies.

Emotional Empaths

The emotional empath is the only type of empath that deals strictly with emotional overload. While saying this, I must reiterate what I have said that you can be an emotional empath who finds themselves gravitating toward another category as well. These categories are not concrete.

The emotional empath has the stereotypical image of the empath throughout the media and across the Internet and popular books on the subject. This type of empath is constantly overwhelmed by emotions that do not belong to them, and they are often labeled as excessively moody, perhaps even being incorrectly diagnosed with bipolar disorder or another mental disorder along the same lines.

Emotional empaths cannot stand to be around too many people for too long. Their constant ups and downs are a direct reflection of the world around them. While they make the most empathic and compassionate friend anyone could ever ask for, they tend to hide away from large crowds, excessively raucous parties, and gatherings of more than five people. These empaths are sometimes found to be in and out of the therapist's office, trying to understand why or what is going on with them, and why they simply cannot get a handle on themselves.

It is not uncommon for the emotional empath to cry in a sad movie or feel extreme emotions that can change according to the mood swing of their surroundings. Music is a great assistance to all empaths, and especially to the emotional empath. Music can be used to trigger a desirable mood if the empath finds themselves in an emotional state when they feel they cannot handle their situation adequately.

Unfortunately, the brain and body do not do well under continued stressful situations. An emotional empath who is in the presence of a narcissistic personality or has a career in a fast-paced overcrowded environment all of the time will find that they continuously suffer from stress overload. This can be remedied through calming music and visualization techniques involving cutting strings to the outside world. It is imperative for the emotional empath to bring themselves to their center point and to use music to make this transition when they are feeling overwhelming emotions.

The emotional empath is also cautioned to look at the material with which they fill their day. For example, if the emotional empath likes to spend their relaxing time watching movies or videos on the Internet, what sort of material are they watching? Horror movies, dramas, or anything with an excessive emotional undertone will be replicated inside the empath. The world around the emotional empath must be designed to alleviate the emotional pressures and reproduce positive emotions. Comedy works excellently in this regard or feel-good movies where there is a feeling of achievement at the end. This sort of emotional injection is like a holiday for the emotional empath.

Physical and Medical Empaths

Physical empaths are sometimes referred to as medical empaths because of the nature of their empathic abilities. Where emotional empaths absorb the emotions of others into themselves and these emotions manifest as the empath's own emotions, the medical empath does so with physical symptoms. The medical empath is sometimes accused of being a hypochondriac as they are always complaining about some or other ache or pain.

Hypochondria is actually only a mental disorder and only coupled with symptoms that the person equates to being part of something much greater and life-threatening (MedicineNet, 2020). If the medical empath is working from their shadow, they may very well begin fixating on the symptoms, and if they are unaware that these symptoms, physical aches, and pains belong to something outside of themselves, they may very well fall into the bracket of hypochondria or somatic symptom disorder (SSD).

SSD occurs when someone's thoughts about their physical symptoms are excessive and constant. They are prone to anxiety and panic attacks. The mental worry about their physical state is beyond any normal stress caused by illness (American Psychiatric Association, n.d.). The difference between hypochondria and SSD is that SSD has actual symptoms where hypochondria does not always occur or has mild symptoms. Many people confuse these two disorders, and the label 'hypochondria' is loosely used to mean anyone who experiences excessive worry about their health or has frequent trips to the doctor.

A medical empath who is not aware of their empathic abilities will be found to own a large medicine cabinet or always have a wide range of medical supplies stashed in many places. They will always have migraine pills with them and may sometimes suffer from codeine dependency. There are many cyclical disturbances within the medical empath which make the diagnosis of such an empath extremely difficult. The more medicine that they use to treat the pain and illness that do not belong to them, the more their minds and bodies will suffer.

The medical empath is urged to analyze their symptoms whenever they arise. It is imperative that the medical empath asks questions of themselves and their pain. They must learn to become in tune with their bodies and find their true state of being, so that when they become ill all of a sudden, they can rid themselves of these feelings and the accompanying physical symptoms.

Unfortunately, the medical empath has an extremely difficult road because physical pain is one of the more difficult aspects to control mentally. It is also extremely difficult to simply understand what pain does belong to you and what pain does not. For the medical empath, the most beneficial physical practice is yoga. Yoga will assist the medical empath with the ability to get to know their body and the energetic vibrations that belong to them and thereby discern what vibrations do not belong to them. The most beneficial form of yoga would be Kundalini yoga, as it will also bring the empath in line with their inner power through the absolute balance of the masculine and feminine aspects of the self.

Claircognizant and Intuitive Empaths

The emotional empath and the claircognizant empath would, under theoretical means, be confused with one another. However, there is a vast difference between the two. The claircognizant empath, who is sometimes referred to as the intuitive empath, feels the emotional, physical, and mental states of another person. This feeling is not an emotional pull and manifestation like in the instance of the emotional empath. The intuitive empath has an inner knowing called intuition or claircognizance. This is difficult to pinpoint because it does not only happen inside the brain or mind, and it also does not manifest anywhere in the body.

The intuitive empath has no physical symptoms, except for extreme fatigue, when dealing with people who are greatly burdened by any extreme mental, physical, or emotional state. The intuitive empath is also prone to fatigue and a drained feeling after dealing with large crowds or visiting a hospital.

This fatigue feeling occurs when the intuitive empath is not aware of how to guard their own energetic system. In general, the empath is pulling information about the world around them. The intuitive empath is overloaded with information that encompasses their entire being. The intuitive center can be overwhelmed by excessive amounts of information when the empath does not shield themselves.

This claircognizance of the world around them occurs through focus. The empath needs only focus on something and the knowledge from this subject, whatever it may be, will be absorbed into their understanding. The intuitive empath is also extremely vulnerable to memories and can pull large amounts of information from past experience thereby draining themselves.

It is wise for the intuitive empath to be aware of what they give their attention to by surrounding themselves with positive items, positively influencing people, and having energy building spaces. Music that calms the being and brings positive vibrations into the space where the empath finds themselves is imperative. The intuitive empath must learn to shield themselves energetically and also understand what shielding does.

Shielding the energy system is fantastic to protect yourself, but the intuitive empath will more than likely have learned to depend on such inner knowing information to meander through life. When shielding, this information is cut off, and although this is fantastic for taking a break, it will also cut the empath off from their purpose and universal understanding. Shielding should be done when going grocery shopping or when needing to be in large crowds for mundane purposes. For the rest of the time, it would be wiser for the intuitive empath to bring balance in their lives between rest, alone time, and spending time in the outside world.

The empath and all those who wish to understand them must also understand that we are constantly 'downloading' information from the universal network. Shielding is one of the first pieces of advice that every single person will give an empath. It is also the fastest way to cut off their connection to the universal source. Rather, find balance, build strength, and find understanding. The intuitive empath is in dire need of a connection to the universal source energy, and without this connection, they will find themselves in a downward spiral.

Earth and Geomantic Empaths

The geomantic empath is one with the earth and is an extension of the planet. They are often exceptionally brilliant at finding anything anywhere. Their sense of direction is unparalleled, and their love for the earth mother is inspiring. The earth empath is sometimes labeled as a hippie or a pagan, and sometimes they are both these at the same time because it is within these labels where they find some sort of comfort.

The earth empath can feel the earth more than any other person. Their affinity toward the planet as a whole is overwhelming and more than often completely misunderstood to those around them. These close friends of mother earth are never at home indoors, and when they are indoors, you will find them surrounded by almost everything that they can collect from outside. They will always have plants and rocks around them, even bowls of water (many times rainwater or sea water that they have collected), and perhaps even feathers and seashells.

This nature loving empath is nonjudgmental about which part of the earth they love the most, and they will hardly ever choose a single place, which they will not mind as long as it is outside. The earth empath also has a difficult time wearing shoes. They have a natural habit of walking without shoes or only with socks. The earth empath is energized by spending time outdoors; however, there is no specific time of day or night, as long as it is not inside.

The earth empath is also a great advocate of looking after mother earth, and they are usually the front-runners in movements to save the planet. The one thing that must be understood about the earth empaths that separates them from other empaths is that they can feel the earth within them. They feel the state of the very ground that they walk on, and they understand the language of the earth as though it were their mother tongue.

The earth empath feels more for the earth than they do for anything else, and earth comes first before everything, including themselves. The earth empath is energized, and their gifts are strengthened by spending time barefoot on the soil, grass, or beach sand. When they are connected to the earth, they are home. To place an earth empath at a desk job is to allow them to wither away and lose sight of their life purpose.

The earth empath is also sometimes confused with what is known as the earth angel. While earth angels are said to be incredible advocates fighting for the benefit of all humanity and the earth itself, the empath is an actual living embodiment of the earth. They are an extension of the planet in such a way that when they are shown videos or images of the earth being hurt, or when they witness acts of pollution and deforestation, for example, they are deeply hurt. This pain is likened to the emotional empath being confronted by the funerals of people.

It is wise for the earth empath to work outdoors and fight for positive change toward the earth, but they must remember to recharge and live in the moment, to spend time in the beauty of nature and to not keep the uglier aspects of humanity's ill regard in their hearts all the time. These sensitive souls need a lot of time outside and they really are the hope of the earth herself.

Fauna and Animal Empaths

The fauna or animal empaths are the animal whisperers of humanity. There is no particular animal that the fauna empaths prefer or who prefers them. All animals are sacred to the fauna empath, and they have an incredible attraction to all animals. There are many people who are compassionate toward animals, but the fauna empath differs in that the animal kingdom is not lesser or greater than they are.

The fauna empath will more often than not have the ability to sense the spirit animals of other people as well. They speak and understand in the metaphorical language of animal symbolism. It is not simply a case of being fond of animals or being able to walk into a house and the resident cat comes to sit on your lap. No, the fauna empath lives and breathes everything that encompasses the animal kingdom. While they do have the ability to understand and feel the mental, physical, and emotional states of all animals that they come into contact with, it is more than simply being a whisperer and caretaker of the earth's animals.

To illustrate the intensity of the power of the gifts inherent in the fauna empath would be a difficult task indeed, however, think for a second about how you perceive the world. When you look at someone, how do you see them? When you think of the stars, what do you see? When you imagine who you would like to spend your every moment with, what is your answer? For the fauna empath, animals are the answer to all the above questions. They truly prefer animals over their human counterparts and will give their lives to help save the animals on this planet.

The fauna empath is, like all empaths, often severely misunderstood and thought to be a crazy cat lady or someone who is an outcast because they prefer spending time working with and being around animals than they do with humans. Even though they are severely misunderstood, their strength lies in spending time with animals. As with the geomantic empath, the fauna empath cannot stand to be without the animal kingdom in their space.

The zoo, to the average person, would be a wonderful place to take the fauna empath to go and spend time with the animals, but this would be one of the worst mistakes that one can make. The zoo is a terrible place for the fauna empath, and they are deeply hurt by the condition in which many animals find themselves. It is as though the fauna empath is in the cages with the animals and they feel their grief, sadness, loneliness, and urge for freedom more than anyone. This inability to witness suffering of any kind toward animals makes the fauna empath the brunt of many jokes calling them weak and silly.

The problem is that the more empaths are mocked and ridiculed for being what and who they are, the more likely they will retreat into themselves and live through their own shadow aspects. The fauna empath is the animal kingdom incarnate. They are the healers of the animal kingdom, and in their spiritual self, they understand animals on a deep spiritual level which incorporate the spiritual and metaphysical truths. A great exercise for the fauna empath, if they are not already well acquainted with the practice, is to learn about animal totems and spirit animals. Fauna empaths also deal better with life when they know what their spirit animal is and have symbolism in and around their homes of their specific totems and spirit animal.

Psychic and Medium Empaths

Unfortunately, the literature on psychic empaths is usually rattled off to mean a general outline of the traits of several empaths together. Psychic empaths are not emotional empaths or telepathic empaths or even precognitive empaths. Psychic empaths are more accurately called medium empaths because they are solely focused on and pick up on the world of those who have passed on and all who exist on the other side of the veil.

Where the confusion comes in is how the empaths express the energetic absorption that they get from communing or experiencing the other side. Medium empaths are either extremely spiritual when they are standing completely in their power, or they are anti-spiritual and refuse to believe anything when they are acting from the shadow self.

It is a tricky business attempting to categorize the psychic empath because they can be seen alongside dreamers and personalities that are "never home" in this world or flighty. They behave in peculiar ways to the social norms and have traits that are rarely accepted. For this reason, the psychic empaths isolate themselves from the world. They also prefer to live alone because of their ability to perceive the other world in such a strong manner that there is no difference between this world and the other side. They are one and the same.

Psychic empaths are not always found in esoteric circles, and many of them prefer not to be associated with such circles because they despise spiritual manipulation and hearsay. The psychic empaths know when someone is talking garbage about their spiritual experiences, and they also find it insulting when people lie like this simply to seem as though they are special. The medium empaths have a difficult life from when they are young because the world in which they live is one that is usually not shared by their parents, siblings, or friends. They almost always have family who can attest to them having imaginary friends when they were little and are described as loners, black sheep, and sometimes as the freak of the family.

All these labels are painful for the psychic empaths and their intimate relationship with the other side either turns to acceptance of spirit and isolation or rejection and multiple failed attempts at trying to fit in with the "normal crowd." The psychic medium feels actual symptoms from the spiritual realm. They have visions, feelings, emotions, thoughts, understanding, or uncontrolled actions. The psychic empath is also prone to vivid and sometimes horrific nightmares, and many of them have insomnia because they have a fear of going to sleep.

The psychic empath is more often than not terrified of the dark. They will sleep with the lights on, and no amount of therapy or acceptance of their gifts will stop this habit. There is the odd exception to this characteristic, but it is very rare.

The psychic empath is also said to be able to sense both positive and negative energies around people. Whether these energies are actual entities, thought-forms, or something else is beside the point. It is within the sensing of these energies where the psychic empath's abilities come into play. They are able to become these energies and the energy of the spirit world manifests directly through them. It is for this reason that many may believe that they are possessed sometimes or have spirits "working through them."

This empath is extremely vulnerable to being unable to exist in normal society if they do not control what they experience. It is wise for this type of empath to learn to guard themselves against negative energies through prayer, spiritual means, and strong visualization techniques. It is also wise for this type of empath to learn to set boundaries with spirits and to have alone time and "switch off" the spiritual bombardment.

In the case of the psychic empath, shielding is important to learn for moments when they need to recharge and be alone. It must be understood that the psychic empath is picking up on spirits all the time, whether they are alone or with other people. This is perhaps the most exhausting gift to carry as an empath, and it is also one of the rarest, next to the Heyoka.

Psychometric Empaths

Psychometric empaths are connected to the universe, just like all empaths are. The difference between psychometric empaths and other empaths is that the former are tuned into the energy in both animate and inanimate objects. Psychometric empaths receive and translate the information that they gather through animate and inanimate objects via a variety of ways. They can either touch an object and have a vision, or they will have a deep inner knowing, or they will have a familiar smell or some sort of physical reaction.

Psychometric empaths are very rare in that they do not only receive information from the living world around us but also pick up the same intense energy from everyday mundane objects. Psychometric empaths are often portrayed in Hollywood movies. They are usually seen as the resident psychic who finds criminals or lost children through the touch of clothing, jewelry, or other special items. While Hollywood portrays psychometric empaths as gifted psychics, and this could be true, they are so much more than simply gifted psychics.

The difficulty for the psychometric empaths lies in the fact that the visions, feelings, emotions, or any other reactions that they receive from the objects that they handle, or the people that they come into contact with, actually manifest in their own bodies. Psychometric empaths are therefore categorized as introverts and will choose to be extremely particular about what they have around them. They will also choose the company that they keep with careful consideration.

Psychometric empaths are usually not the type of empaths that you will find willingly helping someone else out because an uncontrolled experience as strong as what the psychometric empaths feels is usually so overwhelming that they close themselves off to the world. Key advice for the psychometric empath would be to practice mindfulness and begin working on slowly controlling the energy that they receive. To effectively control the energy, the psychometric empaths would be wise to practice meditation. They need to be quiet in their minds so that they can become aware of who they are beyond the energy that they receive and pick up on. While this type of empath is extremely rare, all empaths can hone the skills that the psychometric empath displays.

Precognitive Empaths

Precognitive empaths are people who can see ahead in time. The precognitive empath receives this information about the future or future events through various channels: waking visions, dreams states, emotions, inner knowing, or any of the other empathic channels of which we have spoken.

The precognitive empath does not have a limit on the time frame that they are able to tap into. They also do not have control over the time frame or the information that they receive. It is difficult for the precognitive empath to control the energetic influx of information, and there are very few case studies that can put a concrete separation between intuitive empaths and precognitive empaths. This is also where the problem comes in where many people confuse the intuitive and precognitive empaths. The intuitive empaths have a clear knowledge of the present moment and all that is happening in this space. The precognitive empath differs in that they are energetically tied to the future.

Precognition usually manifests in the dream state. Many people throughout history have claimed to see visions in dreams. The precognitive empath is someone who has premonitions about future events. They are not intuitive empaths, and they are not dream empaths. While there is very little evidence to scientifically prove the gifts of empaths, neuroscientist Julia Mossbridge believes that this precognition is an innate ability found in all human beings (Times of Israel, 2018). She has written a book on her theories and findings, entitled *The Premonition Code*. Mossbridge provides a scientific look at precognition, which she calls a learned skill that can be honed by all. The precognitive empath must remember to take note of all of their visions, dreams, and experiences. It is in recording these visions, dreams, and experiences that the precognitive empath will strengthen their skills.

Lastly, it must be said that the precognitive empath is not simply experiencing what is known as déjà vu. Precognitive empaths have lengthy vivid experiences that are sometimes difficult to distinguish from reality. It is in making contact with these vivid experiences that may make the precognitive empath seek out psychological or psychiatric help. To have knowledge about future events is an extremely useful gift; however, for the precognitive empath, the experience itself can sometimes be debilitating. As I've said, recording these experiences is essential to understanding more about the self, and how to accurately translate what the precognitive empath is confronting.

Telepathic Empaths

Telepathic empaths are empaths who can hear or perceive the thoughts of others. A telepathic empath who is not aware that they are an empath, or aware of the gifts, may have a thousand thoughts going through their mind, and believe that these thoughts are their own. How the transmission of thoughts works, science would love to know. There are many studies that have taken place and continued to take place in the scientific arena of mind-reading (Inside Science, 2018). There really is no concrete scientific evidence that mind-reading is real, but there are many accounts that it does exist. The telepathic empath is fatigued by large groups, just like most empaths are. However, telepathic empaths, who have control over their own thoughts and their own mental workings have the ability to switch off the thoughts of others.

The telepathic empath goes beyond neuro-linguistic programming or apparent guesswork that has often been the academic excuse for such occurrences. While the intuitive empath has an inner knowing of the present moment, the precognitive empath has an inner knowing vision of the future, while the telepathic empath has actual thoughts that manifest in their mind as their own. Unless the telepathic empath learns to isolate their own thoughts through the constant questioning of whether the thought that has come into their mind belongs to them, they will be plagued by mental chaos with no end. It is important for the telepathic empath to practice meditation and to use psychologically formulated mental puzzles to strengthen their mind, as well as spiritual practices to find balance within themselves.

Heyoka—Sacred Clown Empath

The Heyoka empath has its origins in Native American folklore. Within their folk tales, we find that the Heyoka empath is known as the sacred clown or the joker. Evidence further than this seems to be paralleled with the categorization of all other empaths stemming from a collective agreement. The Heyoka empath has been called the super empath or the most powerful empath. The problem with titles like these for the Heyoka empath is that one of the definitive traits has been found to be one of humility. So, to call the Heyoka empath a super empath, a powerful empath, or anything of the sort that makes the empath feel above anyone else causes the Heyoka empaths to crawl back into themselves and isolate themselves from the world. While the Heyoka empath has absolutely no problem being the center of attention and being excellent leaders, there is a very fine line between making them something special beyond the person next to them.

The wisdom that the Heyoka empath carries is that all humanity is one. This means that even the Heyoka empath with all of their gifts and all of their healing abilities that come naturally from within them, believes that they are no less and no greater than the person next to them. This being said, the Heyoka empaths are greatly burdened by the inability to understand how anyone in the world cannot be empathic.

Heyoka empaths also believe in the inherent goodness of humanity. While their innate abilities make them quite an enigma, they themselves believe that the entire world around them perceives and understands the world as they do.

The Heyoka empaths are named the sacred fool because they have the power to bring truth into a situation through humor. The humor that the Heyoka empaths present to a situation in need is not always comical. In fact, the Heyoka empath will more often than not make a fool of themselves so that they can provide another person with healing. The Heyoka empath is also a mirror, a sacred mirror. The Heyoka mimics either precisely the same action or the opposite action of the people that they meet. This is not to say that the Heyoka does this all the time, as they do it when it is necessary.

This sacred teaching through the art of mirroring belongs solely to the Heyoka empaths. They are so brilliant at doing it, that those who do not really realize that they are Heyoka do it without thinking. The sacred practice may be fantastic for others to learn sacred lessons, for the Heyoka empath, this is a great burden. The Heyoka are often burdened by the drastic emotional, mental, and physical changes that happen when they are around other people. While other empaths find it relaxing to be away from large crowds and can handle a small group of friends, for any length of time, though, a Heyoka desperately needs solitary confinement.

The Heyoka thrive in their own company. There is no such thing as being bored, being alone, or wishing to be in the outside world around other people for this empath. They have excessively busy minds, and their thoughts race around their heads all day long. One thing that the Heyoka empath has in common with the telepathic empath is that they can pick up on the thoughts of those around them. This mental busyness of the Heyoka is coupled by a physical busyness. The Heyoka will often be found doing three things at once, thinking about unrelated projects while they are doing these three things, and would be able to carry on a conversation with you at the same time. They are extremely creative individuals in whichever field they find themselves in. This creativity is the Heyoka's channel to express themselves, and to express the wisdom that they carry within. Two of the biggest challenges for the Heyoka are to learn that they cannot change the world, and that they need to look after themselves first. For the Heyoka, self-care is very difficult. They will always place themselves second or third below everyone else around them. The mission, purpose, and reason that they are here on earth is to guide, to nurture, to teach and to provide a platform for spiritual enlightenment to everyone that they meet.

The Heyoka empath attracts everyone who needs spiritual guidance. They have a warm approachable personality and presence about them. The problem with this is that they hardly ever make time for themselves, because each time someone requests something from them, they will not say no. It is therefore advised that the Heyoka empath cuts out a specific time of the day, each day, for themselves. This self-care is imperative for the Heyoka empath to grow spiritually and to download the necessary information from the universe to assist those that they meet.

Unfortunately, in this digital age, and due to the nature of literature on the Heyoka empath, it is not uncommon to find empaths wishing that they were Heyoka. Unlike other empaths, Heyoka empaths are outcasts in society, they are often seen as rude, abrupt, black sheep who run against the grain. You will never find a Heyoka empath being a follower of any social norm. They are the ones who stop the trends but will not follow their own. Their life is chaotic, and more often than not it seems that they are going absolutely nowhere. Their actions and their decisions often make absolutely no sense to themselves and those around them. However, later in life, the Heyoka empath realizes that everything that they have been through, including great suffering early on in their life, is all part of the great role that they play in bringing humanity together.

(You may see that I refer to "empaths and Heyokas" throughout this book as if the Heyoka is not a part of the category of empaths. On the contrary, Heyokas are empaths on a different, more powerful level. Hence why some people call them super empaths.)

Dream Empaths

Dream empaths have an unparalleled connection to the dreamscape. The dream empaths have extremely vivid dreams. Their connection to the dreamscape is apparent just by speaking to them. The dream empaths will make constant references to dreams in normal conversations and will be extremely good at deciphering other people's dreams. Their cognizance of the metaphorical, symbolic language of the dreamscape comes naturally, and this is how they are able to understand dreams without much effort. While the experience itself is very different for every dream empath, they all share the fact that they attest to the dreamscape being another reality.

While I could fill an entire book discussing the dreamscape and experience the dream empaths have in it, I must mention that one of the most beneficial practices that the dream empath can take on is lucid dreaming. There is a vast amount of literature out there to guide the dream empath through the stages of bringing on lucid dreaming as well as venturing through a lucid dream and not being afraid. The dream empath, apart from being a natural lucid dreamer, is also able to converse with spirit guides, lost loved ones, and people who live far away through the dreamscape. Dreaming itself has two important elements to understand: the first being that our dreams are often a dumping ground for that which our brain does not use, or that which the brain finds unnecessary to retain. The second element to dreaming is the space that is inhabited and mastered by the dream empath. It is in this space where possibilities are endless, and it is my opinion that we have not yet been able to document all the prospects that the dreamscape has to offer. It is wise for the dream empath to keep a dream diary, in fact, it is imperative in order for them to strengthen their gifts and harness their skills.

The Myers-Briggs Connection

There is a great connection between what is known as the Myers-Briggs, or the MBTI assessment, and understanding the empathic nature. However, before we dive into the connection between Myers-Briggs and the empath, we must first discuss the history and function of the assessment itself.

The Myers-Briggs assessment, which is one of the most widely used tools to understand the personality of a human being in the world today (The Myers Briggs Company, n.d.), does not actually measure the personality of a human being at all. The Myers-Briggs assessment isolates how one perceives and judges the world around them. It does this through a series of carefully crafted questions, which on the surface seem like average, everyday questions. Each person on earth has a function stack that consists of four cognitive functions found in the Myers-Briggs assessment. A function stack comprises the personal preference isolated within the test. Each function stack belonging to a person has a specific organization. For example, in the perceiving functions, the extrovert in question is stronger in introverted intuition. Their function stack could therefore not include introverted intuition in the next level which is called the introverted perceiving function. To explain this further, the four functions are separated into two groups, the first being perceiving, and the two functions that fall under that are sensing and intuition. The second, judging, has two functions known as feeling and thinking. Each person has an introverted and extroverted quality assigned to a function. Without going into too much detail and overcomplicating the purpose of this explanation, one can understand the Myers-Briggs assessment by likening it to an operating system of a computer. The person in question would be the computer, and the results from taking a Myers-Briggs assessment—your personality type—would be your operating system. It is through this operating system that you function with the world around you. This involves the interpersonal communication qualities, abilities, and desires that you naturally have (James, 2018).

The Myers-Briggs assessment is often said to pinpoint your personality, but it does not tell you how you behave or how you act. Instead, it tells you how you function and how you judge and perceive reality. Therefore, the Myers-Briggs assessment is what exists before you have even come into contact with the world. The Myers-Briggs assessment and literature originated from the work of Carl Gustav Jung, and they were adapted for a broad public audience through Isabel Briggs Myers and her mother Katherine Cook Briggs. The assessment itself took 20 years of development before reaching the public through publication in 1962.

Now let's look at the relationship, or the connection, that exists between the empath and the Myers-Briggs assessment. What I've said before is that the scientific evidence surrounding the nature and existence of something called an "empath" is few and far between, yet through the Myers-Briggs assessment, we can find a common function stack belonging to empaths. It cannot be said, though, that all empaths belong to the introverted, intuitive, feeling, and judging (INFJ) function stack. However, this theory is widely accepted by spiritual communities. The reason for this is that the INFJ personality type exhibits the same traits as those belonging to many types of empaths. The Heyoka empath has two generally accepted personality types. The first of these is also the INFJ personality type, and the second is the ENFJ, known commonly as the protagonist. While I am not going to discuss the Extroverted (E) Intuitive (N) Feeling (F) Judging (J) personality type in greater detail, I am going to discuss the qualities and traits belonging to the INFJ personality type:

- The desire to succeed—Success is important to this personality type. They are always busy trying to better themselves, and their circumstances, and the circumstances of those around them.
- Loathing small talk—Small talk is a waste of time for this personality type, and they crave deep meaningful relationships in their life.

- Giving life or greater meaning—This personality type can often be found wondering about the very nature or meaning of life. Trivial subjects, just like the point above, do not interest this personality type in the very least.
- Pleasing the world around them— This personality type often feels the need to please the world around them. This is one of the more negative traits, especially because this personality type does not make time for themselves.
- Wise beyond their years—People found with this personality type often have a natural sense of wisdom which is not indicative of their age. They are also fantastic at giving advice and being able to sense the true nature of any given situation.
- A lonely world—Because this personality type has a desire to contemplate the deeper nature of existence and form meaningful relationships in their life, it is often extremely difficult to find people who truly share their viewpoints. Therefore, they may find themselves feeling isolated and cut off from the rest of the world.

While these are a few of the traits shared by those in this personality type, there are a whole host of online channels whereby you can do research into the deeper meanings of the INFJ. I must also note that it is extremely important to understand that all tests, assessments, and mechanisms designed to categorize and label are not definitive in assessing whether one is an empath or not. However, if you feel that you are an empath (and it is a deep inner knowing) whether you share the traits and the characteristics or not, you must follow your intuition and your inner knowing first.

Affective, Somatic, and Cognitive

Empathy

The three forms of empathy—affective, somatic, and cognitive empathy—describe the levels of empathy that can be learned by everyone. Of course, the world would be a far greater place if each and every person decided to begin advancing their own empathic skills. With regards to the empath, these three forms of empathy may exist together in the person, or one form might be stronger. It must be noted that every single empath, including the Heyoka empath, will contain skills in either affective, somatic, or cognitive forms of empathy.

Cognitive empathy has to do with understanding. The person who has cognitive empathy as a primary skill in empathy will find that they perceive the world through a mental lens. In other words, when dealing with another person the empath will use phrases such as, "I understand what you are going through, I know what it is that you need to do, I think that the steps that you need to take are...." Cognitive empathy works on the grounds of knowledge. Therefore, someone using cognitive empathy in a situation will draw on their knowledge base.

Affective empathy, on the other hand, deals directly with experience. This is the "feeling by emotion" type of empathic response. Someone using affective empathy will often use phrases such as, "I feel your pain, I feel what you are going through, my heart goes out to you...." While many people take for granted that the empath uses only affective empathy, this is not true. Cognitive and affective empathy are not true reflections of what actually takes place within the empath; they are only descriptions of channels that can be used to partake in the life experience of another person.

Somatic empathy, sometimes called motor empathy, on the other hand, is a mirrored physical reaction that takes place. Somatic empathy is a characteristic almost always found in medical or physical empaths. While the data on motor empathy are far too little to provide comprehensive conclusions, there has been much work around this form of empathy in young children. In fact, cognitive, affective, and motor empathy studies are greater in child studies than they are in adults (Raine & Chen, 2017).

Chapter 2: Solid Signs That You Are an Empath

Before you even begin reading this chapter, you need to understand that the entire foundation of what an empath is has not yet been backed by science at all. There are thousands of examples where the fundamental aspects of the nature of empathy are being studied. Empathy itself is a fascinating topic within the scientific fields, however, it would be difficult to find a single scientist who will bet their career on attesting to the fact that empaths really exist.

The empath has empathy. However, as we have seen in the previous chapter, the world of the empath is filled with so much more than mere empathy. Empathy itself is imperative on earth right now, but the empath brings an entirely new dimension to healing and communication in this digital age. I know, in my soul that empaths exist, not only because I myself am an empath, but because I have met so many other empaths, and I have done so much research to find the scientific correlations that can help my empath brothers and sisters out there. To tell you that science backs the idea that superhuman beings exist, is to lie. Unfortunately, science has acquired a name for itself, where it is held in higher regard by most people than the very intuition that we hold within ourselves. Science is so important to the world at large that we forget what a rich fountain of knowledge each one of us actually is. Many people would rather believe something outside of themselves, irrespective of the lack of evidence, than believe their overwhelming inner truth.

I present to you the scientific evidence that is sound and relatable in the real world. I, too, am guilty of favoring science over hearsay, but through my experience and the experiences of other empaths around me, I have found that when we listen to the small inner voice that the world really does become our oyster.

Can You Relate?

In the section below, you will find a collection of experiences from empaths across the globe. For many of these experiences, the empaths themselves did not want to be mentioned. I have absolutely no problem with this and wanted to add it into the book because I do believe that their experiences will relate to and help other empaths. I will mention where I have added in stories from my own life, and in other spaces I may have changed their names. I have not made up any of these experiences. Regardless of the names given here, they are all very real experiences.

What I want to make very clear about the purpose of this section is that the examples contained herein are for you to become aware of all the instances in your life when you are using your skills as an empath. My entire book is aimed at uplifting and empowering all empaths and people who have awoken the natural gifts that lie within.

I believe that these examples may very well be initiators for your own lightbulb moments. In other words, sometimes we don't realize how much we use our gifts, or we have used them for so long that we no longer recognize when we use them. For many empaths, their gifts are so ingrained into their day-to-day life and how they interact with the world that they are no longer aware of how often they use them. It is also not uncommon for empaths to disregard their gifts as something that naturally occurs and is not special at all. The truth is, and this is what I hope you will find within the snippets of real-life events, that your gifts are truly special and truly needed, especially in this day and age. So, without further ado, let us dive into examples from empaths.

Lost and Found—Our first experience comes from author Amanda Buck (2021). Every year, Amanda went to camp. Her first experience with empathy occurred when she was eight years old. She found that she had an unusual connection to one of the camp counselors, whom she calls Rob. Every emotion that this counselor felt, Amanda felt as her own.

At the tender age of eight, she knew absolutely nothing about empathy, or whether she was just a highly sensitive person who had a great connection with her counselor. Four years later, and four camps of studying this connection later, when Amanda was 12, she speaking with a friend about the situation. A different counselor overheard the conversation. She told Amanda that actually, she was reading a book about that very topic.

As they were talking, Rob was across the field and was looking for something. Amanda and her counselor tried to make sense of what he was screaming across the field. Amanda realized that he was looking for his counselor pack that contained the first-aid kit that he had to always keep on him. Amanda yelled back at Rob, and told him that he had left it in the craft barn. Amanda did not know this personally but due to her connection with Rob, she knew it intuitively. He completely dismissed what Amanda had told him saying that he had not visited the craft barn at all that day, and so it was definitely not there.

Early in the evening, Rob returned carrying his counselor pack, looking sheepishly at Amanda, saying that he had found it in the craft barn, and he had forgotten that he had visited the craft barn earlier in the morning. Amanda Buck writes about many other empathic experiences that she has had throughout her life. It is perhaps these experiences, which under normal circumstances make absolutely no sense to logic, that pushed her career into working for the betterment of everyone around her.

Sadness and Despair—This story is one of my own experiences with empathy. My husband and his dad owned an automotive repair business. One day, when I was pregnant with our first child, I was sitting in the office there and one of their customers came in. I knew the man, as he was an old friend of my father-in-law and a regular visitor. As he entered the area I was sitting, I began to feel an overwhelming sadness and despair. I felt as though I was helpless. I thought to myself, "Why am I suddenly feeling this? Is this mine?" I brushed it off but carefully observed my feelings as if I was an outsider to my own body. "John" sat with me, and we began to talk as we always did. Soon he was telling me about how sad he was feeling for his daughter. She was six months pregnant and had just lost her baby. He said he felt so helpless and didn't know how to comfort her. Now it made sense why I was feeling this way. Finally, I had confirmation that these emotions were not mine. It was my first realization of my empathic ability combined with immediate confirmation. After this incident, I was able to better identify the feelings that were not my own. And with practice, I began to understand the importance of observing, not absorbing the world around me.

Parental Influence—Bella's experience – Bella says that one thing that was truly peculiar growing up was that she remembers having a whole host of illnesses, headaches, and hip pains. She also remembers feeling that her body was an alien. That it really didn't belong to Bella. One minute she would be fine, and the next she would have aches and pains in the most absurd places in her body. It is only when she went to varsity that the symptoms seemed to go away, at least for a while. You see, while Bella was at school, she would visit her mother every day at the hospital where her mother worked. Well, she moved away from home and closer to varsity after school. Here, the only thing she really experienced was frequent bouts of nausea and large amounts of pain in her stomach as though she had anxiety, but nothing like what she had experienced in her school years and living with her mother. It was only after reading that there was such a thing as a medical empath who can manifest the physical distresses of others in their own body that she began to realize what was going on within her. Another realization dawned on Bella, and this one was not pleasant at all. She realized that she did not know her body and how it reacted to her thoughts and to the outside world, even in the slightest.

Bella's life had been so plagued by the physical distresses of other people, and not one of these illnesses, not one of these aches or pains, had ever been hers. After her realization that she was an empath, and possibly a medical empath at that, she began to purposefully learn about her own body and how she responded to the world at large. She learned shielding as soon as possible, and before she even made contact with another person, she made sure to put up her shield. It has taken a lot of practice, but Bella reports that it has been worth it.

The Hollywood Experience—This is something that I have always experienced as long as I can remember. I've always been squeamish watching movies where the character gets hurt.

Whenever a character was injured in a movie, I would put my hand over the same spot on my body and physically react by flinching. I would actually feel a tingling sensation in the same spot as the injury. I never realized that no one else felt the same way. For the longest time, I couldn't watch someone get a serious cut, in a movie or real-life. I felt like I would pass out. As I got older and learned about special effects and make-up, I was fascinated with the artist's ability to recreate realistic-looking injuries. The more I learned, the more I was able to watch more movies because I trained my brain to see it as art and something to appreciate. I began to be critic of the art. Basically, if the bloody special effects do not solicit a physical response out of me, I know it is not realistic enough. Sometimes, people who watch a movie with me get annoyed that I pay attention to the quality of the special effect. But really, it is my way of dealing with the empath in me.

This experience with empathy is generally accepted worldwide among empathic and highly sensitive individuals. This experience also has to do with theory of mind, which is one of the great debates in the world of psychology. Have you ever watched a video or a movie and found yourself flinching, or reacting to the pain that the person in the movie is feeling? While this experience itself is very general, and we would like to think that each person in the whole world feels exactly like this when they watch a movie, they do not. As a child, I never understood why I was the only one flinching. Many people proclaimed that I must be overreacting.

There are some people, in fact, there are more people who do not react to movies or to seeing someone fall and hurt themselves and seeing sights like this does not make them flinch at all. For some empaths and highly sensitive people, this experience can be so traumatic that there is usually one or two genres that they cannot watch, read about, or even experience in any form. One such quick test is to think about or look at someone being cut open slowly with a scalpel. In this scenario, the blood is trickling down, and the person is tearing away...I cannot even finish writing this. The point of the matter is that empathy that belongs to the empath and to the highly sensitive person goes further than just simple face-to-face contact. In fact, it does not have to be a visual scenario that affects empaths or highly sensitive people; it can be a simple thought, or it can be reading something in a book. One of the problems with these experiences is that we think they are funny, or that they have no real effect on us, but the truth is far from that.

When an empath or a highly sensitive person is confronted with a situation like the one described above, their body goes into a stress response, and they feel everything, mentally, physically, and emotionally as though they were going through the experience themselves. Therefore, with an experience like this, if you do relate, then it is wise not to subject yourself to such scenarios – whether this means that you must cut out a few new movie nights with friends, or not read those books that make you sit on the edge of your seat, or perhaps you need to stop surrounding yourself with scenarios that make you feel depressed, anxious, stressed, or any other negative emotion. If you relate to the above scenario, and there is anything that you cannot watch, or something that makes you flinch and turn away, then you need to stop subjecting your body, mind, and emotions to such scenarios. You will only be happier and healthier for leaving these experiences behind.

Sleeping to Dream—Joanne's experience – Joanne reports that people have described her as someone who can sleep for days on end. She has absolutely no problem falling asleep or entering lucid dream states. She also has a peculiar frequent occurrence in her life, where people she has just met will tell her about their dreams and ask her to decipher the meaning behind them. Joanne has never read a dream book that explains meanings in her entire life. She has just always had this deep connection to the dreamscape. Dreams for her are not just average occurrences that we go through, they are a deep integral part of our existence. A few years ago, Joanne realized just how powerful the dreamscape truly is. While she has had many experiences where she has seen what will happen the next day in her dreams the night before, she had never experienced something quite like this. In her dream, she was sitting in the passenger seat next to her aunt, and they were chatting away like they always do, when a red pickup truck swerved in front of her, and she woke up.

Although she thought the dream was very peculiar, she could find absolutely no meaning in it, especially because her aunt was not in town. Well, sure enough, Joanne went to work and at 11 AM, she received a phone call from her aunt to tell Joanne that she was outside, and that they should grab a bite to eat. Joanne realized that she had again had a premonition, and so she begged her aunt to sit at the café across the road and not drive anywhere. The aunt was not the type of person to listen, and she definitely never believed in any spiritual hogwash. She couldn't leave her meeting and, unfortunately, she never saw her aunt again. This was one of the most difficult experiences of Joanne's life. Not only did she lose the deal in her meeting, but she lost her aunt too. While she has had so many other experiences, Joanne says that this one taught her that human life is far more important than any other monetary nonsense.

The Boss—My boss and I were at a district meeting. We sat next to each other in a small room with a large number of people. As the meeting progressed, I felt anxious and panicky for what seemed like no reason at all. I looked at my boss and whispered, "Are you okay?" He looked at me, got up, and left the room. He texted me from outside the room. "I can't go back in there. It's too crowded and I was starting to panic." I knew then that what I was feeling was *his*, and not mine.

Not Perfect, Just Empathic– Anne Marie's experience – Anne Marie feels that people in her family and so-called friends think that she is perfectionist but she thinks there is no such thing as perfect. People around her have said that she takes people on as projects to try to fix or change them but that's not the case at all. She just feels so deeply and being an empath, she attracts these kinds of people.

Also, she tends to think aloud asking if the energies are her own or from someone around her. As she essentially "talks to herself," she asks if she needs to change herself or let those feelings pass. In turn, people observing her perceive it as complaining verses her way of problem-solving through her empathic experience. Anne Marie feels that in the end we are only accountable to ourselves and for ourselves. As empaths, we need to only take on what we can handle. We should take the knowledge and power from higher beings and spirit guides and remember to keep the balance by grounding ourselves. She says we should help others in their journey whenever possible.

Ditching Law Practice Altogether—I went to law school and became a lawyer. I originally wanted to go into family law. I did a few cases in family court and realized that it was weighing so heavily on me. No one ever wins in family court, and when children are involved, it's worse. I was not able to sleep at night. I would obsess over these cases in my head. I felt so much empathy for my clients that I was willing to sacrifice my sanity, money, and time to help them. I had to start setting boundaries for myself. Eventually, I just left the entire industry.

It was too much for the empath in me. I did not yet know how to protect my energy or shield myself from the clients' emotions.

Absolutely Drained—Kevin's experience – Kevin says that he doesn't remember much about being this bad when he was a child, but in the past five to ten years, he's started to realize that he cannot cope with life anymore. He will find myself waking up in the morning being perfectly capable and even excited for the day ahead. Some mornings he will wake up with a thousand thoughts in his head about what he's going to do for the day. He is an incredibly organized person, however, his life and the way he is living it does not reflect this even slightly. Whether it's on the telephone or if he has to go out to buy groceries, the second he has any contact with anyone, he feels he must sleep. If he doesn't sleep, even if it's a 30-minute power nap, he is the grumpiest person alive and an absolute horror to live with. It's almost as though his brain switches off and becomes something else. However, he has recently noticed after much research that he identifies with some traits described by other empaths. When he became aware that he was sleeping so much, almost running away from his life, he realized the peculiar feeling of having a heavy, almost crippling weight on his shoulders. When he woke from his nap, this feeling would be gone. Through searching for answers, he realized that this feeling was that he was picking up energies that were not his own. He has since tried various meditations to bring him back to feeling himself again, and while it is not perfect yet, it is a solution which has provided him with a lot more time in the day and more happiness throughout his day!

The Material We Surround Ourselves With—In college, I wrote a 30-page research paper on The Jewish Holocaust. Specifically, I researched the worst concentration camps—

Auschwitz and Dachau. In my research, I watched videos, looked at pictures, and read many detailed firsthand experiences of the atrocities. After a few weeks into the research, my fiancé finally said to me, "Can you put that down for a week? It's really affecting you." It wasn't until he said something that I noticed how depressed I was becoming. I was feeling so deeply for the people in these camps that it was like all the life had been drained out of me. I had to put the research down for a while and come back to it later.

Sensitive Child – I have always been told that I am extremely sensitive. As a child, my mother described me as such. I could always *feel* when my mother was mad at me. I would beg her, "don't yell at me!" even though she never actually yelled. I believe I just felt that she wanted to yell but because of my sensitivity, she had learned how to speak to me in the calmest voice. I could still *feel* her frustration. My mother had to tell my teachers how sensitive I was because they did not understand the intense emotional input that I received from all around me. In first grade, I even chose to move my seat to the corner because I could not concentrate sitting with my classmates around me. Whether I sat in the front, back, or middle of the classroom, I took in so much from around me that I was distracted. The teachers were baffled that I would choose to sit in the corner but it worked better for me. I thought it was normal to be able to feel so much from others. As I grew up with just my mother and I in the house, I did not realize that I felt every bit of her sadness, depression, anxiety, and more. I thought that we were just extremely close at heart, because we were, but me being an empath is what made us closer.

The Magic Touch—Steve's experience in his own words – "Some time ago, I felt like I discovered a super power. I could seek out the aches and pains in my wife's back or leg just by touch. At times it is the worst super power as I can easily find the most sensitive parts and as I'm not a trained masseuse I can't really fix it or I apply to just a bit too much pressure and cause her to yelp. More often than not though, I can localize her pain and gently massage it out. My empathy is strengthened by our bond, but I think I've also been able to detect other people's pain without ever seeing or even touching it."

Bullying Thoughts – I was picked on a lot as a child and teenager. Back then, it wasn't dealt with at the adult level. My mother tried to teach me methods of standing up for myself against them. Bullies were especially tough for me to deal with in high school. I could feel their detestation as I walked by them, even if they just looked at me and said nothing. Walking by people through the school halls, I would always feel how their day was going. I could also feel when someone was perceived to be a hard-shelled person by others, but was really just a sensitive person themselves. I became friends with many of those people as I could feel their true character.

Positive and Negative Aspects of Being an Empath

While this seems to be a New Age culture that believes that being an empath is akin to being a superhero, not everything about being an empath is positive. The act of empathy itself is imperative to the well-being and the future of this planet. And while I believe that empaths are here to lead this global transformation and teach others about the importance of empathy, I also believe that the core reason that we have so many empaths coming forward to be *exposed*, for the lack of a better term, in the public eye, is because they are carriers for the core emotion of empathy. Empaths have a heavy burden, and as an empath myself, I cannot tell you how badly some days I wish it wasn't part of me. At the same time, I have a deep love for humanity. I believe that I share this deep love for humanity with all empaths and Heyoka. Without empaths, I don't believe that empathy would have found such an important front seat in the world of science today.

Sitting in this front seat in the world of science, true empaths have a great responsibility to the rest of humanity. While there are thousands of blogs, articles, books, and information strewn across the world, including a multitude of different opinions about what an empath is, I believe it should not become something that people strive to be. Being an empath and having empathy, as I've said before, are two vastly different things. It is imperative that the entire world comes to a place where an empathic response to life is the norm. There are claims that all people are empaths, and even though this cannot be proven, I am highly doubtful. Until the empath is completely certain of who they are within, they really live the life of people around them. The life of the empath requires learning to pass through the various stages of becoming oneself while still experiencing the rest of humanity. The empath is sometimes akin to being a superhero, and while this could be true, the empath must be willing to put in the hard work and use many years to find the core aspects. In my chapter entitled, Tools and Suggestions for the Empath, I provide other empaths with real-life tools and suggestions to successfully assist others around them, in addition to the necessary tools and guidance to find themselves.

Empaths were not born with a manual to explain the ins and outs of how to meander through this world, how to heal people, or how to deal with the constant influx of emotions, physical manifestations, thoughts, visions, and dreams. *What Is an Empath?* hopes to be the manual to guide and to assist and to nurture all empaths and Heyoka alike back to their core being by removing the frustration and by providing well-researched, first-hand experienced information and guidance. So, before we dive into the guidance and how to really manage life successfully as an empath, let us look at the positive and negative aspects that we carry.

Positive Aspects

- Great Intuition—All empaths and all Heyokas share the natural intuitive abilities. This is not to say that people who are not empaths or Heyoka do not have intuition, because each person alive today has that inner compass that they can connect to. Empaths have a stronger ability from the get-go. Empaths do not need to gain this ability, just practice it; the intuition is already there. Their intuition is usually extremely strong from when they are little, however, this great intuition can also one of the negative traits that all empaths share. Allow me to explain. The empath must learn to listen carefully to their intuition, give it the respect that it deserves, and form a strong trust with the messages that come through. There are many people who complain and say that once listening to their intuition that they were led wrong, and so they do not trust this intuition in a voice any longer. There is so much in our minds that can distort the intuitive messages that it takes time and patience to be able to be accurate.

- Powerful Healers—Empaths are naturally powerful healers. Depending on the type of empath, healing occurs in a variety of ways. Heyoka empaths heal by being a mirror to other people, and through their unique sense of humor. All empaths, and Heyokas included, provide the sacred space for healing to occur by simply being in the situation. Of course, it depends on the situation as to the nature of healing that occurs. Another important factor to remember is that empaths do not heal per se. Instead, what they do is similar to what counselors do in a therapy session. Empaths provide the space, and the person in question heals themselves. Empaths alleviate the pain, share in the emotion or mirror the situation, and by simply being themselves, they bring the person in question into a place of awareness where healing can occur. Despite the large amount of literature across the globe that claims that empaths remove energy from people that they are with, this is not the case. An empath lightens the load by sharing in the experience, by climbing in the boat with the other person, and literally standing in the shoes of the person or people that they are with. It is in this shared experience where the empath brings out the best healing possible from the other person.

- **Immense Creativity—Heyoka and empaths alike are extremely creative.** This creativity expresses itself in every area of life. It is a common mistake to think that creativity is synonymous with art—painting, sculpting, drawing—when creativity can be found even in the most analytical of jobs. The empath and the Heyoka show their creativity through expression in areas of life where they are the happiest. For example, an empath who is in the nursing field will give 110% more for their day jobs, and they will find new ways to make the experience better for everyone around them. Creativity is defined as "the ability to produce or use original and unusual ideas" (Cambridge Dictionary, 2021). It is through this understanding that we can see how the empath and the Heyoka alike are able to be creative in absolutely any field. Their creativity also comes naturally to them because they are able to sense the needs of the people around them through their specific gifts.
- **Deep Relationships— both empaths and Heyoka look for and commit to deep relationships.** Whether these are friendships, romantic relationships, or what could be classified as cosmic small talk, the empath will always seek out interest in deep meaningful social interactions. This means that an empath could never be happy in a relationship where there was no commitment, or with someone who was shallow, superficial, or whose conversation was skin deep.
- **Masters of Compassion—Empaths are the masters of compassion on earth.** It is the gift that they bring to this planet in order to bring about positive change and radically alter the face of the earth for the rest of time.

Unless we are speaking about dark empaths, there is no situation where an empath will be accused of being uncompassionate. It's not that an empath shows mere pity to another person, a mere sympathy. The dictionary definition of compassion is "a strong feeling of sympathy and sadness for the suffering or bad luck of others and a wish to help them" (Cambridge Dictionary, 2021a), and empaths take this a little further. The compassion that they show would be combined with *empathy*, as a strong feeling of empathy and emotion for the suffering or bad luck of others and a wish to help them.

- High Dedication—When an empath finds something that they believe in, they are dedicated wholeheartedly. If an empath is invested in what they are doing, regardless of whether the thing is part of the life purpose or not, they will give absolutely everything to see that what they are doing, or what they are part of, succeeds. Empaths are among the most driven, dedicated individuals on the planet.
- Very Understanding—When it comes to understanding people, there is nothing that bypasses the empath. Regardless of how the empath absorbs information, they are able to completely understand everything about the person, animal, or situation that they are dealing with. This is why, given the proper theoretical knowledge, the empath outshines everyone else in what they do. There are specific careers that are naturally tailored to suit the empath such as counseling; more about that in Chapter 9.

Negative Aspects

- The world seems overwhelming—The world of the empath is constantly being bombarded by information. It does not matter if the empath is awake or asleep, they are constantly receiving. It depends greatly on the type of empath to understand how they are overwhelmed on a constant basis. However, for the empath or the Heyoka, there is really no downtime. Spending time alone, in nature, or just away from large crowds is a wonderful way to take a break and re-energize. However, even in these places, there is constant receiving of universal information.
- Extreme Loneliness—While one of the negative aspects discussed above is opposite to the one being discussed now, for the empath they really go hand-in-hand. While the world of the empath is constantly being bombarded by information, they feel more alone amid the energetic

buzz than mere words can explain. If an empath, or a Heyoka, spends time with other empaths or others who are like themselves, they do tend to find meaningful relationships. The time it takes to find another meaningful relationship can take years. In some cases, empaths grow up in families where they are the only empath. Through their youth, they are molded by being branded as the black sheep. They carry this loneliness well into their adult years and only after much introspection and many years of isolation do they realize who they truly are. This is perhaps one of the most imperative reasons why communities of empaths are necessary. It is also why gentle, straightforward guidance is needed to reach people and families who have empaths in their midst.

- Confusion—It is very rare to find an empath who does not understand a state of confusion: Confusion about the world, confusion about themselves, confusion about what an empath really is, and confusion about what is going on inside them and how to properly use their gifts. Even if an empath has honed their gifts, they know what it the state of this confusion feels like. This confusion can lead empaths down a multitude of different paths. They will chop and change throughout their lives, their careers, their choices, and partners and friends, until they learn more about who they are and what they are capable of. Confusion particularly affects empaths because of the amount of information that continuously overwhelms them and permeates every part of their existence. Turning this confusion into a quest of self-exploration and information about the world is the way to empowerment.

- Solitude and Self Isolation—As discussed in the bullet point above (Extreme Loneliness), empaths truly understand what it means to feel lonely inside. However, this loneliness does not stem from their choice to self-isolate. Empaths love their own company; it is in this space where they are all by themselves that they recharge and find true meaning to what it means to be alive for them. The most extroverted empaths love spending time with themselves. Many people will see them as introverts; however, if an empath does not make time for themselves, they will suffer from burnout. Solitude may seem as though it is a positive aspect, but in today's society it is not. It is difficult for the empath to socialize and be part of a buzzing world all the time. For example, an empath working in marketing, even for the most honest of companies, will constantly suffer from anxiety, burnout, panic attacks, and sometimes even bouts of depression. This is not because empaths are not capable of being the most remarkable marketers, especially because they know exactly what the audience needs. It is because a demanding career such as marketing requires constant attention, constant focus, and an empath cannot deal with a career like this.
- The Self—One word that you would never think would be in the same sentence as an empath is the word selfish. However, many empaths have been labeled self-centered, selfish, or self-absorbed. It sounds absurd, the main purpose for the empath is to serve their fellow humans. This misconception comes about because the empath is constantly on a mission to better themselves, to find out more about themselves, and to understand the world in which they live. It is very natural for the empath to use only themselves to benchmark against,

and this is because empaths are nonjudgmental and will always choose to use themselves as guinea pigs. Empaths are not self-absorbed, selfish, or self-centered. They are simply born into a world that does not have a definition for them yet, and so they have no concrete guidance as to how to properly navigate this world.

- Saying No—The word 'no' does not feature in the empaths' vocabulary. Until the empath learns to set boundaries and how important saying no actually is, they find themselves tearing out their hair trying to keep promises that they have made to keep the whole world around them happy. Empaths do not want to disappoint, and this is not because of guilt, or any feelings attached to that negative emotion, it is because they can sense how the other person will react to the word no. For the empath, one of the first and most important exercises is to practice boundary setting. Of course, this does not come easy, and will cause the empath great distress at first, but if they do not set boundaries they will never learn about their true selves.

A Discussion on the Aspects of Being an Empath

The examples above may not have been based on scientific lab-found evidence. They were, however, based on the consensus and experience given forward by thousands and thousands of empaths. The information presented is also based on my personal findings, and so it is not a bible describing what an empath is or what it is not. In this life that we live, there are so many things that exist that we do not know of yet and that we do not have concrete evidence for, and yet they exist, without even our awareness of them.

My example to illustrate this better is to imagine a person who has unbreakable, unshakable faith in something. But you cannot see it and you cannot perceive it. Therefore, in your frame of reference, in *your* world, it does not exist. Similarly, the importance of humanity is defined by us. We have nothing to compare ourselves against, as there are no species that threaten us, and because of our limited understanding, we define ourselves as the most advanced species on earth. Therefore, by self-definition, we are intelligent, even though we share a 1.2% genetic similarity with the chimpanzee (Smithsonian Institute, n.d.). In every scientific field, there is still so much studying that needs to happen for us to get a complete understanding of who and what we are and what our place in this universe is. Humanity loves arguing facts, and even the grand String Theory is no longer applicable in the face of quantum physics. It is for this reason that you must reach within to understand the fundamental truths of your own being. If something is true to you, and it is not causing harm to yourself or anyone around you, then you need to accept this truth for what it is. No amount of science should sway you because the life that you live belongs to you. The experiences that you have belong to you and to absolutely no one and nothing else.

The examples that I provided you with may seem common or able to exist in everyday life. If this is your thinking, then you are an empath or a highly sensitive person. The peculiarity of empaths and highly sensitive people is that we really believe that the entire world thinks like us. We tend to believe everyone cares about everyone else, just like we do. Unfortunately, this is not the case. Although, the world is not some big bad place, and even in saying that perhaps I have a little positivity bias (but that is a discussion… and another book).

The relatable examples have a purpose in where you may find yourself in the words and sentences. They also cover both the positive and negative aspects that are found in empaths, as well as highly sensitive people. One thing that I ask you to be mindful of when you digest the information that you have read, and in fact when you read the entire book, is to trust your own inner voice. I want you to trust yourself before you trust anything else because you are the master of your own life. And while we may need the tools of the cosmos to come to grips with who and what we are, in all these mathematical pattern-making tools for categorizing each aspect of human existence, is the still small voice within that holds the key to everything that you are, and every truth that you seek. Searching is important in defining ourselves, and looking for new ways to understand ourselves is imperative. However, while we do this, while you read everything that is contained within these pages, I ask you, please listen to what truly resonates with who and what you are, and not what you wish or aspire to be. We will speak about authenticity and its vital importance in your everyday life a little later in the book. Now, if you are not already completely authentic with who and what you are, then please put on your authenticity cap and read on…

Chapter 3: Scientific Theories of Empathic Abilities

Throughout the various scientific fields, empathy and its relevance have resulted in a growing body of empirical research. While there is still a large amount of speculation, great headway has been made in proving the existence of active empathy. The Greek root word of empathy means "feeling into" (Pallipedia, n.d.), and interestingly enough, it was the German philosopher and psychologist Theodor Lipps who brought the origin of the use of the word into something akin to how we use it today.

Empathy was originally thought to be the human expression of feeling into inanimate objects. For example, if you could look at a piece of artwork and connect with it, you were practicing empathy. Any inanimate objects, artwork, even a stone sculpture that evoked empathy from a person would be seen as a success. Theodor Lipps found that empathy did not only extend toward inanimate objects but also from person to person, and between a collective group of people (Montag et al., 2008).

Empathy has since traversed throughout the psychological landscape and found itself in every corner and on the lips of every therapist and counselor. Within the study of neuroscience, empathy still has an almost firm standing in the theoretical landscape. I do believe that once we prove the existence of empathy across all scientific fields without doubt and be able to accurately measure it, we will begin the journey that explains the inner workings of the empath.

Yet empathy is the study of the century, and empaths still find themselves belonging to pseudoscience. Psychology understands empathy, and has many places for the possibility of empaths, but if this is not coupled with neuroscience, if this is not coupled with hard science, then we cannot say that we have a definitive scientific explanation. As an empath and an author, I would love to pick up a journal article and reference the success in the scientific fields finding the reason for empaths holding the gifts that they do. Unfortunately, this is not possible yet. What we do have at our fingertips is an exhaustive supply of thousands upon thousands of studies dedicated to finding the origin of empathy. We also have a great many studies that show what happens when empathy is present alongside the darkest of human traits. I discuss this in greater detail in Chapter 7—The Connection Between Empaths and Narcissism.

For the sake of this chapter, we will look at the areas of science that are dedicated to finding the connection between empathy and the human mind. It is important to remember that as vast as the universe is, so too is the mind of the human being.

The Mirror Neuron System

All humans are soft-wired with what is called mirror neurons. Scientists have found that all primates are soft-wired in the same way. But what is this whole mirror neuron business that has fascinated the scientific world since the early 1990s? The science of mirror neurons states that if you are having any sort of emotion, heightened or not, and I have the capability of experiencing that same emotion, I will mirror your experience in real time.

The whole mirror neuron concept is what lies behind the empathic drive for humanity to naturally want to belong. We are not soft-wired to be apart from each other, we are soft-wired to fit into the rest of society. This may seem ridiculous if we look at how humans behave, however, this is exactly what science shows us, and according to research, this is only the beginning of understanding why humans behave in the peculiar ways that we do.

From early childhood, in fact, from our first conscious moments where we observe the world around, we are learning through observation (Lancey, 2021). This does not stop at a certain age and continues well throughout adult life. Up until the discovery of mirror neurons, scientists believed that there were only two types of neurons found in the nervous system. These two types of neurons are known as motor neurons and sensory neurons. Motor neurons deal with action and reaction, and they cause movement by sending signals from the brain to various parts of the body. Sensory neurons on the other hand are responsible for things like temperature and pain.

Mirror neurons also found in the nervous system, and evidence suggests that they start developing before the age of 12 months. Scientists have suggested that it is the mirror neurons that are responsible for imitation and observational learning (News Medical, 2019). The science itself is still in its infancy stage, and while many reports have claimed that mirror neurons are the only thing behind empaths and the gifts that they exhibit, the science has yet to be proven.

Mirror neurons are fascinating though, in that they prove that the point and purpose of the empaths is fundamental to our core human aspects of social interaction. A review in the *American Journal of Psychology* on a book by Gregory Hickok titled, *The Curious Book on Mirror Neurons and Their Myth: The Real Neuroscience of Communication and Cognition* shows precisely why I refuse to make any claims on mirror neurons or neurons with the mirror mechanism present (Rizzolatti & Sinigaglia, 2015). I am not a neuroscientist, and while bookshelves and the World Wide Web is booming with claims on what these neurons and neurons like them are doing and are responsible for, I refuse to take an intellectual stand to confirm or deny their role in the presence of the gifts that belong solely to empaths. Judging someone else's experience, especially when there are so many vast and different valid experiences, is inappropriate. And perhaps, although fascinating, this is why the empath is also so difficult to study scientifically.

What I will take a stand on is that I think it goes a lot deeper than what the scientific evidence has come to understand. A book on empaths and for empaths would not be complete without the section. However, I promised from the very beginning that I would only deliver the truth and so I must declare that there is not yet enough substantial evidence to prove or disprove that mirror neurons are responsible or even connected to the gifts which belong to empaths. The evidence does suggest that these mirror neurons are connected to the act of empathy. However, as you will come to see, if you have not already, empaths are about far more than the act of empathy. And while the scientific world debates through lengthy acts and painstaking hours of research about whether the mirror neuron theory is correct or not, or whether mirror neurons are even present at all (Lingnau et al., 2009), I would rather we stick to what we know through experience and through day-to-day evidence. I do believe that while I wish that science would find a solution or a categorization for empaths and empathy itself, humanity is far too quick to jump on a sentence from a journal discussing a new discovery to substantiate their own claims. If scientists have not come to a conclusion yet, how can we?

Emotional Contagion

Another interesting concept that has been around before the discovery of mirror neurons is that of emotional contagion, which is defined by The International Society of Substance Use Professionals as "the ability to influence the emotions and behaviors of others, either directly or indirectly" (2017). It is surmised that mirror neurons are responsible for emotional contagion. Emotional contagion is also wrapped up in how we learn and how we adapt into socially accepted behavior.

The entire reason why you believe certain things are right and why others are wrong is because of socialization. You are taught the act of socially accepted behavior through emotional contagion. While emotional contagion only touches on influencing thoughts and feelings, we are more susceptible to these nonverbal acts, and we learn far faster and far more than we realize through them. This automatic response mechanism is built into us from birth and permeates all of our existence. The entire theory of emotional contagion allows us to understand why it is so important that we are mindful about who and what we surround ourselves with. You definitely become that which surrounds you, like birds of a feather.

It is extremely possible that highly sensitive people are subject to greater levels of emotional contagion than others, yet it still does not explain the psychic elements attached to many types of empaths.

Electromagnetic Fields

As Dr. Joe Dispenza was quoted saying, "[S]cience has become the new language of the mystical" (n.d.), the scientific proof for the electromagnetic field that surrounds each and every person is not substantial enough to prove that it exists, yet there is enough evidence to prove that something exists.

Human beings have managed to measure a wide range of energetic fields that disrupt us and our health, yet we have not yet been able to pinpoint the size and magnitude of the human electromagnetic field. We have also not been able to accurately define the electromagnetic field that connects everything in existence. Small studies, such as the one done by Stapleton, Dispenza, and others, have been able to show an increase in energetic response through the use of the Electroencephalogram (EEG).

When I speak of a small study, I speak of 223 novice meditators and a total of 5,616 EEG scans. In this study published on October 27, 2020, it was found that there was a great significant change between premeditation and post-meditation of every single one of the 223 people who partook in the study (Stapleton et al., 2020).

Spiritual teachings have spoken about the power of the heart and how it is the epicenter, even being called the seat of God, of all human interaction. However, with signs being the new language, the millions upon millions of spiritual practitioners and empaths must wait until science catches up and finds a way that is simpler and easier to measure the powerful electromagnetic field which Dispenza states is the space in which we create our entire existence from and through.

According to research done by the World Health Organization (WHO) and their agenda for electromagnetic fields research (1997), electromagnetic fields (EMF) have always been present on earth. While the WHO is desperately concerned with the negative impact that electromagnetic fields have on the present and future state of humanity, through their studies, they allow us to understand just how prevalent electromagnetic fields are.

The WHO has found that at low frequencies, EMFs simply pass through the human body. However, the higher the frequency, the greater the risk becomes, and even at radio frequencies, EMFs are partially absorbed and have been found to penetrate the tissue of the body. The WHO has also confirmed that low exposure to frequency fields emitted by mobile phones or even base stations do not cause harmful effects, but they do have an effect on the human body.

When we come to terms with the fact that all life consists of energy and energy in itself is simply information, then we can understand that the electromagnetic field is not so far-fetched. We do understand, through science, that various electromagnetic fields exist around us, pass through us, and affect us. We also understand through spiritual teachings that words carry frequencies, that our very thoughts are energy and carry frequencies of their own. According to the findings of Dr. Joe Dispenza our thoughts influence the electromagnetic field around us. Our thoughts also cause change within this electromagnetic field, and if the change is substantial enough, they change our very lives. While his work is still in its infancy, he has changed thousands of people's lives through his scientifically based methods of manipulation of the energy field that connects all existence. Some of the changes include people who have gone into complete remission from stage IV cancers to people who have come out of suicidal dumps.

Now what does this have to do with empaths? Well, it has everything to do with empaths and the gifts they bring to this world. The empath, I believe, is born completely aware of the connection to the great electromagnetic field of existence. However, when we grow up, we forget this connection because of a whole host of reasons and throw ourselves into a state of confusion. There really is no way to sidestep this, unless the parents of empaths are completely prepared and have every tool in their box ready to raise a healthy, completely functional empath with their gifts intact and still explain reality to them. This sounds like an impossible task, and until science catches up, empaths are all left to find their own feet.

Synesthesia

Joel Salinas, an American-born Nicaraguan Assistant Professor of Neurology at Harvard Medical School, writer, and researcher, has spoken openly about his experience with the type of synesthesia known as mirror-touch synesthesia. According to him, he became truly aware of this neurological peculiarity when he was in medical school. Salinas witnessed a man receiving CPR, and at the same time he felt the pressure on his own chest. Everything the man went through, Salinas physically felt within himself.

There are many types of synesthesia, and one type that correlates closely with emotional contagion and the fascinating function of the mirror mechanisms found in the body is mirror-touch synesthesia. Sounds and colors are interchangeable with touch and taste. Music can play in one's mind while observing a child swinging in the park. Synesthesia happens when more than one sensory system or cognitive pathway is stimulated instead of one. Information is not confused; it is rather increased across platforms within the body. It is said that those who are born with synesthesia make up 5% to 6% of the world's population. Some have called it a sixth sense, some have called synesthetes gifted, and there have been claims that empathy may be connected. The most common form of synesthesia is called the grapheme-color synesthesia. This type of synesthesia is connected to color, the synesthete associates color with various aspects such as days of the week, numbers, or even emotions. The existence of synesthesia just comes to show how vast the neurological landscape is and how much room there is to discover about our true potential.

Chapter 4: The Spiritual Theory—Energy and Psychics in the New Age

The whole world is awakening. The whole world is experiencing life. There is a shift in the depths of each and every human being. The intensity of the shift is dependent on the soul work done by the person. We will discuss soul work in greater detail in the next chapter. In this chapter, I will give you an outline of what the New Age spiritual revolution has done for humanity. I'm also going to show you exactly what the spiritual gifts are and how your inner compass plays the biggest part in guiding you every step through life.

The New Age spiritual revolution has opened the doors to the radical acceptance and acknowledgment of all spiritual paths. Indigenous cultures have found a new lease on life and humanity, at least the spiritual community at large, and they have found that the mundane world is simply not enough to carry us through each and every day. From Shipibo shamans to the art of Dadirri, from the origin of the goddess to the understanding of Christ-Consciousness, we have so much spiritual literature at our fingertips that we cannot simply ignore it.

In this world of duality, in this world of hot and cold, every beauty has its dark secret, and the brightest light casts the darkest shadow (Scott, 2012). We cannot understand one side of anything without the other, without its opposite. Similarly, spiritual theory in this digital age speaks of the darkness and the necessity for it. Apart from the art of deep meditation, we build our personalities and ideas of ourselves and the perceptions we hold about the world around us through comparison. It is for this very reason that the spiritual world and its many communities are littered with charlatans. I will discuss these types of people and their importance in this chapter as well. However, this chapter is not about what is wrong with our vast network of spiritually awakened beings, it is about the immense potential for growth that lies within it.

There is so much wisdom to be digested and there are similarly a billion personalities each with their own opinion about what works and what does not. Even I have my own opinions about what has worked in my life and what has not. I learned a long time ago that what is right for the goose may not always be right for the gander. It is for this reason that I'm not going to tell you what is right or what is best practice within the spiritual world. But I am going to give you an overview that holds many years of experience, research, and personal findings.

Within this chapter (and let's face it, with this whole book), I ask that you look for that which resonates with you. If something jumps out of the page, or you feel some sort of sensation while reading any of the information in this chapter, or in this book, understand that it is a calling to delve deeper. This is one of the core characteristics of using your intuition correctly. I'm thinking that you, my reader, are either an empath on the road to seeking answers, or someone who knows an empath and is also seeking answers. The commonality is the archetype of the seeker. We have many archetypes that make up who we are and while Carl Gustav Jung founded this theory on archetypes, it is our revolutionary present-day Mystic, Caroline Myss, who refined them for modern-day spiritual travelers (Myss, 2015). There are thousands of archetypes and according to the in-depth work of Myss, but we have four primary archetypes that belong to the collective and eight archetypes that belong to us alone. Many people have written extensively on the psychology behind archetypal wisdom; however, Myss' work is written and designed to be integrated into one's life alongside a spiritual awakening. To illustrate the power of archetypal wisdom, I am going to share the four primary collective archetypes with you below:

The Saboteur

The Saboteur archetype deals with everything that sabotages your own life and the lives of the people around you. You can ask how something like this could be useful and that would be a good question. When the Saboteur is working from its light aspect, and you have managed to balance your archetypes, your Saboteur will show you places in your life where you could be sabotaged.

The Saboteur has to do with everything from procrastination to laziness, even having anxiety attacks and canceling appointments or running away from situations that would otherwise benefit you. Many people's Saboteur archetype is working from the shadow aspect. In the shadow aspect, the Saboteur, which would normally allow for positive change in all areas of life, would now throw away entire careers, or make you believe that you're not good enough for what you have now. When people are sitting in the shadow aspect of the Saboteur archetype, they will chop and change careers, life decisions, friendship circles, and almost every aspect of their life.

The Saboteur is a built-in survival mechanism. The only problem is when the survival mechanism is used against you. Have you ever stopped right before a major change in your life?

Have you ever walked away from an opportunity and looked back and thought how could you do something like that? This is the inner Saboteur. Of course, the work of the Saboteur is far greater than that. The Saboteur is deeply ingrained in every area of your life. When we refuse to ask for help, even though we are drowning, that is the Saboteur. When you know you have a deadline, but you end up going out, that is the Saboteur. When you believe you can't do something, even though you have all the tools at your disposal, that is the Saboteur.

So, what exactly is the reason for the Saboteur if it closes every door of success? Without the Saboteur, every part of you could flourish if you weren't afraid. This archetype brings out the worst in you so that you cannot identify the best parts of yourself. Each time you utter the words, "I could never do that" and you have no reason to believe that you could never accomplish it, it is the Saboteur within that is showing you that you are being controlled by fear. Those who are afraid of the outside world, afraid of what everyone will think of them, have a shadow Saboteur far greater than they realize.

In the world of the empath, the Saboteur archetype shows itself through doubt, through embarrassment, and through self-worth issues. The Saboteur also shows itself in the life of the empaths when they refuse to put themselves first. It is wise for the empaths to begin working closely with the inner Saboteur and bring it to light so that they can use the tools of the Saboteur for the greater good. Advice from this archetype is to put yourself first, to know that you are worth it (not just think that you are because someone said so), and to follow your own inner guidance coupled with the greatest strength that you can muster. Your inner Saboteur, dear empath, should be your friend in recognizing those that would hurt you or stand blocking your path to greatness. The only way that you make the

Saboteur your friend is to begin to face your fears and start to realize that you are worth it, and that you are more than enough.

The Victim

The Victim archetype is closely related to what is known as the Victim mentality. Unfortunately, the Victim archetype is one of the most debilitating archetypes to come to terms with when we have been through something traumatic. Trauma is a vast subject, and the Victim archetype sits right at the heart of the pain that is done to us.

When we hold onto past situations and are filled with revenge or regret, we are sitting in our Victim. The Victim allows us to heal, but we need to know when it is time to get up, dust off, carry on, and leave the past where it belongs. The Victim teaches us to forgive, learn, and ultimately understand that even the most vicious of experiences belong in the moment that they happened. Trauma should not be carried with us for the rest of our lives, nor should it engulf every moment of our existence. This is difficult to understand, especially when you are in the situation, or the situation has happened very recently. However, forgiveness is key. Even more than forgiveness, the Victim teaches us that we are more than our collective experiences. We are taught through this archetype to stand in the shoes of others and comprehend that not everyone is alike.

The Victim archetype is probably the most difficult archetype to break into the light with. It is not that we must break free from the archetype; instead, we must break through with the archetype. There is much wisdom to learn from the Victim, especially in showing us that we should not victimize others.

The Victim archetype teaches us to be stronger, to be wiser, and to understand that we can stand up out of the darkness; that we can rise up from the ashes. All we need is the willpower and the inclination to allow our experiences to unfold no matter how hard it seems. All we need is the time to heal by sitting in the Victim, integrating and understanding the lessons from life, and then getting up and knowing full well what we never want to experience again. The Victim is an ally in showing you the places in life where you yourself are being victimized and where you are victimizing others. The Victim is strongly tied to grief, to sadness, to bouts of depression, and to an attitude that says, "poor me." When you realize that you are far more than that, you will see that there is a time to grieve, and there is a time to let go. Neither are easy, yet there are some of the most important lessons that you will ever learn in life.

The Prostitute

The inner war between the light and dark aspects of the divine Prostitute archetype are between financial gain and spiritual cost. The Prostitute archetype will sell you and your talents repeatedly for absolutely nothing. This archetype is closely related, if not the sole governor of self-esteem and self-worth. This archetype also defines the identity and the importance of your own belief of self when facing the world.

Do you stand up for yourself? Do you believe in your own work? Do you think that you are worth more than you have right now? Many artists, writers, and creatives have great shadow prostitutes, and they work tirelessly for little to no money while creating absolute masterpieces. When a creative or an empath is working through the shadow aspect of the Prostitute archetype, anger and depression will linger in almost every project they undertake. The Prostitute archetype allows you to understand when you are being taken for a ride in any area of your life. So, you know that what you are doing is worth far more, but if you do not believe it and you do not stand up for yourself, the Prostitute will teach you that you will remain where you are, doing the same thing until you die.

While the Saboteur highlights the fear aspect, the Prostitute shows you that spiritual work and a spiritual life coupled with happiness is exactly what you are seeking. When we run after money, shiny things, and the latest trends, we do not fill that inner hunger. The Prostitute archetype builds your integrity, exposes your true morals, and will either break you or build you. You must know who you are and be proud to be everything that you are at your core. You are born with a specific purpose. You are born with gifts and talents that must be used to fulfill the mission and the heart's desire. When the Prostitute archetype is lurking in the darkness, you will never see the light. This archetype teaches us that we cannot be everyone's friend, we cannot please the world, and you will not be everyone's cup of tea. It is impossible to create something that suits every personality on this planet. You must learn to find your type of people and to flourish within the areas that hold place for your gifts to grow. Do not sell yourself short, and always create from your soul.

The Child

The Child archetype is the inner child. There are many different types of Child archetypes, namely: the Magical Child, the Wounded Child, the Divine Child, the Orphan Child, the Nature

Child, the Eternal Child, and the Dependent Child. The Child archetype is missing in many adults today. There is no free time, no playtime, and absolutely no wonder left in their lives. The Child archetype makes us understand that not one of us ever really grows up.

Wouldn't it be nice just to throw away adult things, have someone else pay the bills, or simply go on a vacation (holiday) and swim in the sea, forgetting about all the stress and worries that adult life brings? In the hustle and bustle of this digital age, we are so busy trying to fight to earn a few more hours of sleep, or pay off that debt, or reach another deadline, that many of us have told our inner child to go sit in the corner and be quiet. Parents no longer have the liberty of true parenting because they are fighting too hard to make ends meet. Gone are the days when children themselves can play outside in the streets, and youngsters are trying to grow up faster than in any generation before this one. As a result, the Child archetype is scared and hiding in the corner, throwing tantrums and believing that life is quite unfair.

The Child archetype teaches you to have a childlike wonder in the magic of the world and to afford yourself playtime, rest time, and allow the work to be done in work hours. When we ignore the inner child, we age faster, we become miserable, and we lose sight of the magic contained in experience. When we lose sight of this magic, we lose sight of the lessons. If we cannot see the lessons, we do not learn anything. If we do not learn anything, each day becomes another day in the mundane cycle that never ends, except in physical death. Without the Child archetype, there really is no one single day in life that holds happiness and happiness is the true aspiration of every human being. Children do not care what adults think of them, until we teach them to care. Similarly, we too must forget what the adults believe, perceive, or judge. We must truly love the life that we live, and to do so we must truly experience each day as a new day. The Child archetype will teach you to love the sunset again, to find hope in the sunrise, to dance under the moonlight and to take time to do what you find pleasure in. What do you truly enjoy doing? Do you even know? Have you explored your likes and dislikes in depth? The Child archetype will remind you in the most creative ways that you are living this life for you and no one else. Remember, that's not selfish, that's self-love!

Spiritual Gifts and Psychic Intuition

There are many spiritual gifts that belong to the empath. Psychic intuition is the umbilical cord that connects the empath to the divine. These many spiritual gifts are given to the empath throughout their life at specific stages of awakening through their psychic intuition. One can imagine that the body is like a computer and the spiritual gifts are the software that allows the empaths to create and fulfill their purpose here on earth.

The great energetic field of universal energy that surrounds each human being and all of earth and the cosmos holds every spiritual gift that you can imagine. Throughout history, humans have attempted to map out all the spiritual gifts such as discernment, faith healing, knowledge, divine wisdom, charity, and intercession. Unfortunately, spiritual gifts cannot be pinpointed or mapped because there are just too many, and the Divine Universal Energy is just too vast for us to even think that we could possibly begin to understand it.

What we do have are many holy books that have wisdom and guidance toward living a life that is more beneficial to the community and the individual. The spiritual gift that is attributed to the empath is, of course, empathy. However, it goes beyond this in understanding that the empath is first, a channel or an intermediary between divine understanding, compassion, empathy, wisdom, and guidance. Then, they are a light to the world and its future. According to shamanism, and many indigenous cultures, we have an umbilical cord that connects us to the Great Spirit. With that umbilical cord, the psychic intuition channel downloads specific spiritual gifts when they are needed and in precisely the correct amount. Those with the gift to see into spirit have attested to a light blue line connecting the spiritual channels. It is through this channel, or umbilical cord that we communicate with Divine Universal Energy.

Some people have more than one spiritual gift that they are aware of. Others are not aware of any of their spiritual gifts, even though it is plain to see that they do possess many. Spiritual awareness is vital in understanding how you communicate with spirit or universal energy to the rest of the world. When you isolate your mode of communication, you will become aware of the time when the downloads happen, and of why they are necessary. You will begin to see how they mold you, and through this awareness, you are able to ask for divine guidance when it's needed and this channel for the psychic intuition will become stronger and clearer the more you work with it.

Prayer strengthens this connection. Meditation is a form of prayer, and the more you work in divine guidance, the more you will grow in balancing your archetypes and bringing your entire being into a space where you are working in the light. Downloading divine guidance is not always glitter and sparkles, as sometimes it hits harder than any human being can, because divine guidance always works with truth, and it knows exactly what is needed at any given time. The empath understands this connection deep within themselves. Regardless of their belief system, they are closely connected. Sometimes the world gets in the way of this pure channel, and the empath falls into darkness. All that is needed in a time like this is introspection and simply talking to the divine, universal energy and asking for blessed guidance in love and truth.

Chapter 5: Religion and the Empath

I believe clear-cut boundaries stifle the growth of the empath. We live in an age where the past rules and regulations no longer fit the freedom that the Divine Universal Energy is bringing into this world. Religion is clear-cut. It marks the beginning and the end and gives the human perspective on what the divine really is. There is nothing wrong with religion. Some people find peace in strict boundaries of belief. But religion holds space for judgment of those who do not belong to it. There is so much beauty within religious texts, and there is so much wisdom contained in the stories of religious leaders, martyrs, and saints. All religious paths hold wisdom. Perhaps each one of them holds a few pieces of the great puzzle, and if we were only to accept them all for the teachings they hold relevant to now, we would have a greater understanding of what Divine Universal Energy truly aspires to create upon the earth.

The truth of religion is that no one knows precisely what the truth really is. There are so many wars caused by religion and opposing faiths, differing opinions, and different names for the same deities, that religion has earned a terrible name. The generation of youngsters that is emerging now on this planet are soon to become adults and have no time for this. Indigenous ways of life have found a new voice in an age that should've killed them off altogether.

It is easy to hate religion and what has happened in the past, but if you think back to the lesson of the Victim archetype, then you will understand that forgiveness is key. Then if we move onto the Saboteur's lesson, we realize that change is perhaps vital to the progression of spirit within a religious context. Freedom of speech and belief where no harm is caused to any living thing is the motto of many an empath's heart. Empathy exists at the heart's intention of the leaders and martyrs of religion. When we look at the reason behind the teachings of the people that religion holds high, we see no power-hungry scripture, there is no wish for the attainment of material goods, and finances are hardly ever spoken of.

What we do see are teachings that speak of love, kindness, forgiveness, understanding, and advice to communicate with the spirit as often as possible. Each religion has a different name for the same thing. Prayer is contained in each religion and spiritual path, for there must be some practical way the person is to communicate via spirit. When we forget our true selves and believe that we are only flesh and bone, then we are prone to see only the atrocities committed by religious sects. Within the core of all religious teachings lies the inner sanctum of truth. This inner sanctum is where empaths find greater peace and can exercise their gifts and truth to self without condemnation. The inner sanctum is the mystic belief system connected to religion. It is the path that was traveled by saints and mystics, and it is their teachings that formulate the wisdom of inner sanctum understanding.

Billions of people still believe and still follow human teachings, without looking for the inner truth within themselves and within the religious teachings. A mystical path, such as the one that St. Teresa of Avila walked, is not a path that can be defined within a single chapter. Mysticism, regardless of the wisdom that you choose to integrate on your path, asks you to be completely, 100% true to yourself and loyal to Divine Universal Energy. It asks that you walk the path of purpose in faith, just as so many have done before you. One of the more prominent, and yet most debated over persons who understood this truth, was Jesus Christ of Nazareth. Following a mystic path does not mean that you have to carry your cross to your death. However, it does mean that you can accept the wisdom without judgment and find, within yourself, renewed hope for your fellow human.

Empaths cannot thrive in a space where they do not have the liberty to be everything that they can be. Because science has not yet caught up, and we do not have concrete evidence to show that psychic gifts are the work of a divine connection, some religious belief systems may stifle the positive growth of the empath. It is important then, for the empath not to hate or to despise any religious path, regardless of how primitive belief systems may seem. Instead, a mystical path is suggested, and an understanding that is greater than that which we meet at face value. Every moment is sacred. Every word of every mouth from every person has the potential to be defined as a spiritual experience. In fact, divine, universal energy flows in and out of everything, animate and inanimate objects. The energetic field that connects everything permeates all of existence. How can we then believe that something is incorrect or powerful enough to work against the intention of the divine? Through perceiving the world like this, we are able to partake in any religious action and find divine guidance in the words of the most clear-cut boundaries imaginable.

Perhaps it is the work of the empath to revolutionize the image of spirit contained within religion, and manifest into the world the divine truth that empathy lies at the heart of what many call God. Perhaps it is the great work of the empaths to shine light in the darkness that was once the cause for great separation. Perhaps it is part of the divine purpose of the empath to bring an understanding of universal equality and greater unity with compassion into the hearts of humanity.

Chapter 6: Empaths and the Law of Attraction

Because empaths have a natural connection to the world around them, regardless of the way they do this, they are natural agents of attraction. This isn't always positive, and it does not always follow a preplanned path and there are not many empaths who have figured out their own "rules of engagement" with their own law of attraction.

The law of attraction is so much more than a vision board. It is so much more than the World Wide Web has made it. The human being is so much more than we understand. Our human minds are so complex, and there is still so much space for us to make incredible new discoveries in. There are many who would attest to knowing the true secret of the law of attraction, and then there are those who would completely deny any force or agent involved in the preplanning of events. Is there concrete evidence supporting the law of attraction? No. Again, those who are not equipped to speak about the in-depth scientific understanding that we have in this age, are quoting science and finding bits and bobs of information here and there to somehow make their philosophy of universal truth more believable.

Without the science, or the lack thereof, we do know that there is something connecting us. It is more apparent in the lives of empaths and in how they experience day-to-day life. It is extremely apparent in how they conduct themselves after understanding that they are empaths. In some empaths' lives, there is a complete shift when the mind shifts. And the empath who has awoken to their own gifts will attract people who need them. Almost every empath believes that what they go through is what everyone is going through, and this is hardly ever the case. We spoke about the psychic intuition in Chapter 4, and it is believed that it is this channel that allows the empath to manifest and mold their lives the way they see fit. When the empath is acting from shadow aspects of their being, this psychic intuition is tarnished, and attraction is no longer positive but the downward negative spiral.

What Is the Law of Attraction?

It is said that the origin of the idea of the law of attraction comes from the words of Helena Petrovna Blavatsky (1831–1891), the founder of the Theosophical Society and a woman who brought the wisdom of Tibet and the secrets the world's most mysterious spiritual paths to the public eye (Theosophy Downunder, 2008). And then in 2004, Rhonda Byrne, (originally in collaboration with Abraham Hicks, who pulled out of the project) brought about a book that sold over 34 million copies entitled, *The Secret*. In November 2020, Rhonda brought out another book published by HarperOne, promising:

> With every step you take, through this book you will become happier and your life will become more effortless, fears and uncertainty of the future will no longer plague you, anxiety and stress about your daily struggles or world events will dissolve, and you can and will be free of every form of suffering. (USA Today, 2020)

The law of attraction states that through thought alone, your life can change drastically. This thought is by exercises like affirmations, vision boards, and living a life as if the desired change had already occurred. The law of attraction has indeed changed many lives, and there are many people who attest to the miraculous information contained within Byrne's book. I have not read the second one, so I cannot comment on the upgraded knowledge that claims to relieve all suffering from humanity, especially in a time where a global pandemic holds us hostage.

Personally, I prefer the teachings of Abraham Hicks over the publications by Rhonda Byrnes. Abraham Hicks is a collaboration of Esther and Jerry Hicks and "Abraham." Esther Hicks is a woman who goes into a meditative state in order to receive communication from Abraham, who is described as "a group consciousness from the non-physical dimension" (Abraham-Hicks Publications, 2021). Esther does not call this act "channeling" but more of a translation of information into a language we understand. I urge you to seek out the teachings, even you do not believe the source of that which flows to Esther. These universal teachings promote positivity, well-being, self-love, and happiness. One of the teachings is that you are a creator who creates life with your thoughts. (Abraham-Hicks Publications, 2021). Abraham Hicks goes into detail, expanding on the how and why this process of being a creator of your own life works. I believe anyone using this method properly will see the workings of the law of attraction more clearly.

As many people that are for the law of attraction, just as many are against it. There is an energy, which I've spoken about at length, which permeates the world. It is my personal belief that this energy moves through us all and is the inspiration behind the law of attraction. However, being an empath myself, I do understand that there is universal divine timing. Abraham Hicks does a wonderful job of explaining divine timing in more detail in relation to the law of attraction and your inner being. If we were to understand and practice the inner workings and exact methodology behind the law of attraction, maybe every empath would change the lives of every human. Maybe we would be able to feed the nations. We could collectively uplift the downtrodden. Perhaps we have the solution in hand for the elusive world peace but we are just not practicing it. Is it the practice of the methods and not the methods themselves that are imperfect? We are closer to understanding the divinity within us all that we have ever been, but there is still a long way to go before we can make claims about ending the suffering of all people. Please don't get me wrong, the work that Byrne accomplished with her team of experts changed the world. This change was necessary to allow humanity to believe in themselves and their gifts again. While thought has been found to be the most powerful agent that we have to change our lives, Dr. Joe Dispenza has proven that it is more than just the head controlling what happens in your life (Dispenza, n.d.). We have to start somewhere, but there is just so much more to it than reading one (short) book.

In the next section, I will show you how to find balance, as an empath, and empower yourself to attract positive results in line with your desires most of the time. There is no concrete solution that will solve every single problem in life today. We do not yet have a method that is flawless, but what I can give you is guidance along the lines of the law of attraction that worked for me.

A Guide for the Empath on the Law of Attraction

Humanity is so busy thinking of a solution to rid the world of all its problems that it forgets the heart. The empath is so ingrained in this thinking process, and what is right and wrong, what is socially accepted, while still being overwhelmed by the emotional aspects that come hand-in-hand with being an empath. The empath is closer to the inner workings of the law of attraction than anyone else. The reason for this is that the empath understands heartfelt compassion and empathy firsthand.

Perhaps I should first define what I mean by the law of attraction. To me, this means that every part of ourselves is geared toward a desire, this desire becomes a goal. When we use this law of attraction, we need to understand that by thinking about something and having a feeling about it, we attract it. However, there's a catch. If you want something but you doubt that you will get it, you may attract the lack of it instead of the abundance of it. Why does this happen? It happens because the entire being (inner and physical being) is not in line with the goal. One part of us may be completely geared toward achieving that which we want to achieve, and if even the smallest part of us is against it, it will fail. Now that sounds like a headache, and one can think how on earth would you gear your entire body, your cells, your organs, your very skin to be in line with the goal that you wish to achieve?

Simply through the act of heart and mind coherence. Dr. Joe Dispenza has revolutionized the way that science, specifically neurology, has come to see the importance that emotions hold within the life of any person. While he has extensive research, and thousands of testimonials, including those that have returned from stage IV cancer, there is still no concrete body of evidence that gives us a roadmap that will work every time for everything. The goal here is not to find a blueprint that will mark the road out for us. The goal is to find a happy balance in life and to find that space that says that you are allowed to achieve precisely that which you desire.

This is where I believe the book by Robin Byrnes missed the mark. When we concentrate solely on financial gain, and we forget completely about the intricate workings of spirit within us, we lose the magic that claims to be held by the literature behind the law of attraction. Your emotions and your mind control your life. These two 'brains' are driving every incident, every illness, every experience that you have in your entire existence. You are indeed the master of your life, and there is no such thing as someone else controlling the wheel. However, to remain within the driving analogy, you need to learn to drive properly before you can get from A to B. So how do we learn to drive properly? How do we learn to steer our vehicle in precisely the correct direction of our desires? For empaths, the guidance is a little different than the guidance that would be given to someone who is not a natural empath.

Finding the Core Self

For the empath, it is imperative to learn how to get to the core aspect of the self. This does not happen in a single day, and it is very dangerous to think that it will happen within a year. It takes time, especially for the empath, and hard work on the self to find and isolate exactly who and what they are. The process of finding the core aspects of self involves meditation, personality analysis, spending time alone, and extreme levels of authenticity. Because the empath has such an overwhelming influx of energy from the world around them, it is not uncommon for them to believe that they have found their core only to find that these were aspects belonging to someone else. Now we cannot go live in the mountains, or in a cave in Tibet, (I mean, I guess you could) as we need to experience the real world and we need to be social beings. This needs to happen because we need to follow our purpose.

So how would the empath go about reaching the inner depths of truth about self? It all begins with a promise. This promise is made to the empath and the empath alone. No one ever sees this promise, no one ever knows about it; it is a deep and lasting pact that is made between the soul of the empath and the experience of life. This promise states, "I swear to trust myself always, and never to go against how I feel or what I believe to be true." With this promise in hand, the stage has been set and the empath may no longer act unless they feel so compelled. The promise also prohibits the empath from distrusting the self, which, in itself, causes such great harm to the gifts of the empath. This is the first step for the empath, and a tiny disclaimer states that the empath should never break a promise with their soul.

Balancing the Heart and Mind to Work as One

The heart of the empath is extremely strong. Empaths have a natural affinity to be described as heartfelt people. The care and empathy that comes from the empath are so powerful that it can heal great wounds, both psychologically and spiritually. The mind of a normal human being can have anywhere between 70,000 thoughts a day, while the empath is known to have thoughts from others and a cognitive influx of energy from the world around them, so it would be interesting to know what the numbers in the mind of the empath look like.

For the law of attraction to work for the empath, there needs to be a complete coherence between mind and heart. The head needs to trust the heart and vice versa. When we feel something, it is usually our mind that steers us in a different direction. It is very rare that someone naturally is listening to both the mind and the heart at the same time without any conflict. The usual process involves jumping between emotion and logic, and instead of sitting in either one of the two, the empath needs to sit outside of them both. What does this mean? It means that the empath needs to get out of themselves and act as an observer in their own lives. This method is only attained through stillness and deep levels of meditation. When the empath becomes the observer, a unified solution between the mind and the heart can be found. Both logic and emotion can be viewed almost like a courtroom. And instead of the heart or the mind running the show, it is now the empath working from their core self.

Live the Life of Choice

The next step in connecting the empath with the law of attraction is to design your life to make room for the life you want. Your inner being knows what you want. You just need to prepare yourself for it. We have conditioned ourselves to live for the rest of the world and put our own needs last. The empath understands this because they live mostly their entire lives in the light of helping others. You need to take the time to recondition yourself to what you want to attract in your life.

So, the empath lives a life that is rarely ever dictated by choice. For the law of attraction to be more effective in the empath's life, the empath must put themselves first. How difficult is this for the empath? Extremely. There are really no words to explain how difficult this hurdle is to overcome. Life is strenuous enough for the people around the empath, and all the empath really wants is for peace in the world. The empath must come to realize that when they put themselves first, they are stronger and more able to help those around them. Apart from standing up for themselves, the empath must dictate their own schedule that works around them, not around the rest of the world. Second, the empath must surround themselves with people and items that mirror the life which they want.

The people who surround the empath must be supportive, kind, and understanding of the path that the empath walks on each day. If the empath surrounds themselves with people who constantly judge, belittle, or break the empath down, then there is no chance of connecting with any positive part of the law of attraction. It is also imperative that the empath not surround themselves with people who are energetic vampires, because one of the most important things for the empath is to conserve the energy as they spend so much of it on the world. As for the items, a vision board or images, sculptures, wall hangings with quotations and even the books displayed in their home and living space must be geared toward the same desire that they are reaching for. Overall, the empath needs to surround themselves with people and items that promote positive energy and are conducive to goal attainment. This is good advice for anyone, right?

Chapter 7: The Connection Between Empaths and Narcissism

Before we begin this chapter and explain the connection between empaths and narcissists, we must look at the definition of narcissistic personality disorder (NPD). We define NPD as a "pattern of grandiosity, need for admiration, and lack of empathy per the *Diagnostic and Statistical Manual of Mental Disorders*" (Psycom.net, 2021). Narcissists are all about the I. Everything that they do, everything that they are, revolves around them.

By understanding that the narcissist is, and understanding what the empath is, we see they are two sides of the same coin. The empath is the giver, nurture, caregiver, and will focus on providing time, energy, and basically everything that they have to the world outside of them. The narcissist is the taker, the rule maker, and the one who never loses an argument, ever! The empath is the fantasy of the narcissist. Why? Because the empath will listen to their lies and provide them with the love and support that their inflated egos crave. The narcissist is the nightmare of the empath. Why? Because the narcissist can love nothing outside of themselves enough to be seen as remotely giving unless it benefits the narcissist.

NPD goes far beyond my explanation above. There are even four subtypes of narcissists, including the cognitive or cerebral narcissist who believes that they are smarter than the rest of the world; the narcissist who obsesses over physical appearance and who believe they are the lawmakers on what is beautiful, trendy, and considered physical perfection. Then there is the covert or vulnerable narcissist, and this one is a tricky narcissist to pinpoint. Their shyness, and introverted mannerisms make them look like someone who is simply sitting in their Victim archetype. And last, the spiritual narcissist, the one who uses spiritual truths, to control others and to place themselves on a pedestal and appear they are the bearers of the only truth.

Identifying the narcissist is a tricky, sometimes dangerous endeavor and is not something to be done by the empath alone. If an empath recognizes any of the warning signs below in anyone that they know or are close to, then seeking professional help is imperative. The mental damage caused by the narcissist, regardless of the subtype, sometimes takes years to repair. A relationship with the narcissist will bring the empath to their knees, believing that they are nothing without the narcissist, and even though the empath knows in their soul that this is not true, they will continue to give, they will continue to stay. Is this madness? Not for the empath, because they believe in second chances. Empaths believe that wherever they are, they are required to help and heal for the greater good of all humanity.

How then can an empath walk away from a narcissistic relationship? With the guidance of someone who is well educated, such as a psychologist or therapist who specializes in work such as this. With this, empaths can have any hope of coming to terms with the fact that there are some people who do not care at all about anything but themselves. The narcissist to the empath is too bad to be true. An empath who finds themselves in love will fight the world around them to protect the narcissist even though they are being abused down into the ground. Everything on earth has its kryptonite, and the empaths' kryptonite is the narcissist.

What Is the Dark Empath and Why Do Psychologists Fear Them?

Narcissism is largely an enigma and something to be wary of. However, there is something more disturbing than the narcissist. The dark triad comprises three distinctive personality traits: narcissism, Machiavellianism, and psychopathy. We have covered narcissism and its lack of empathy. Let us look at the other two traits that make up the dark triad. Machiavellianism is found in a person who has absolutely no regard for their fellow human beings, and there is a serious absence of moral action or understanding. They are callous, cruel, and have only their own interests in mind. It is best understood that someone who is diagnosed with a personality trait of Machiavellianism is deceitful, manipulative, and indifferent to everything around them. They cannot be swayed, and their unemotional stance allows them to stand on the surrounding people without batting an eyelid just to get ahead.

Psychopathy couples almost nonexistent impulse control with exploitative tendencies and a complete defiance of anything lawful or socially acceptable. The psychopath is usually violent and holds great social assertiveness. They have no regard for close relationships, and have a sick, twisted desire for destructive thrill-seeking.

This combination, this suit of destruction, is known as the dark triad. Psychologists, therapists, and counselors know that there are people who possess this personality profile. However, there is something more terrifying, more destructive, and more devastating to the life of the empath than the dark triad personality. This destroyer is known as the dark empath. The dark empaths differ in that they are the dark triad coupled with empathy. They possess enough empathy to coax the world around them, and to hide their viciousness and cold disregard for life in general. The dark empath is not only kryptonite, but they are also certain death to the empath and the empaths gifts. They will use and abuse the empath until there's nothing left for them to gain. Once this is done, the dark empath will have no use for the empath and will throw them out to the wolves. There are people who believe that the Heyoka is the only weapon against the dark empath, however, this is simply hearsay. It is wise to learn the art of being able to let go. The empath must learn to let go of small things and repeatedly practice letting go. It is useful to begin practicing with thoughts alone; if you could let go of thoughts and do this continuously then you will be strong enough to let go of the more difficult things in life.

Recognizing the Warning Signs

There are many warning signs showing the narcissist's true colors. I have added the most pertinent signs for you to be aware of. If, at any time you are faced with someone who fits three or more of these signs, then it would be an excellent idea to get professional assistance to guide you through dealing with a situation like this.

- Narcissists have an inability to say sorry. They have a troublesome time apologizing, and everything that they do is always right. A narcissist cannot be wrong even if they are.
- Narcissists cause those around them to believe that they're going crazy, or that their memory is acting up, or that they have completely lost the plot. A narcissist will cause those that they are in relationships with, be they formal or romantic, to lose themselves completely. Someone who is involved with a narcissist will not be able to remember when last they made their own decisions.
- A narcissist requires consistent flattery, validation, and attention. Those who are around the narcissist will need to continuously praise what they're doing and the strengths they perceive to hold. The narcissist will never tarnish their reputation on purpose, and they will protect it with their life.
- Anger comes easily to a narcissist. They are sore losers. And when they are subject to narcissistic injury, they will become a raging ball of insults.
- Narcissists have no empathy. Unless you are dealing with a dark empath, the narcissist will be able to deal with issues and situations without lending a helping hand or showing any remorse or compassion. The true narcissist is unable to feel emotions connected to other people or anything outside of themselves.

- The narcissist is extremely charming. They can charm the pants off almost anyone, and they do. Everything is about them and how fantastic they are. These stories, which they have a multitude of, will be told in repetitive cycles, each time emphasizing how dangerous the situations were, how they were the hero, or how they were victimized repeatedly. Everything the narcissist tells you will evoke emotion.

Chapter 8: Is it Mine or Someone Else's?

Before the empath has awoken to their gifts, they will experience many thoughts, emotions, and perhaps even mood swings. Before an empath knows they are an empath, they are often diagnosed incorrectly with disorders such as bipolar disorder. Not that every person who has bipolar disorder is incorrectly diagnosed and is an empath. The trick to understanding whether the feelings, thoughts and experiences belong to the empath or not is for the empath to understand precisely who they are.

The constant energetic influx of information overwhelms and fatigues the empath. Through exercises, which I will discuss in greater detail in Chapter 9, the empath will find themselves, to understand what makes them tick, and will realize foreign energy manifesting in their own body. Recognizing the energy that does not belong to the empath is paramount to living a life that is constant and positively progressive. The empath must be willing to put in the hours and the hard work in order to function optimally while making use of their innate gifts.

The empath must also understand that all situations do not serve their life positively. There are indeed people in this world who will do things to lift themselves up, even if that means destroying another person—narcissists come to mind. However, people like this do not need to be narcissists to destroy another life. Negative energy manifests in a million different ways and one failsafe manner in which to recognize negative energy is to know how to listen to your body.

Your body is akin to a satellite dish that picks up all the surrounding frequencies. All this information is passing through you. However, when it directly affects you, as in a relationship, your body will send warning signs. If you are not aware of how your body reacts to different situations, you will not understand the messages that it is sending you. It is therefore important for the empath to know themselves so well that they understand the language in which their body speaks and who they are at their core.

Empaths have a peculiar trait of attracting people who feed on the energy of others and people who love dumping their responsibilities, problems, and emotional baggage on the empath. These sorts of people are not healthy additions to the life of the empath. It is in the empath's nature to be okay with being a punching bag. Regardless of the type of situation, the empath needs to realize that every person comes from a different walk of life. Everyone doesn't feel or care the way the empath does. It is only through awareness that an empath can recognize when someone is dumping all their nonsense on them. It is not the responsibility of the empath to take care of the world at the expense of their own wellness. The empath must learn to take care of themselves first.

It is also common for the empath to find themselves in situations where there is so much happening that they are in over their heads. This is one of the negative traits, and it is difficult for the empath to say no. There is only so much that any person can deal with before they are subject to burnout. If the empath does not learn to set boundaries and to learn to say no, then they will have a tough time living life positively. Life is not meant to be a struggle, and especially for the empath, life itself is meant to be a joyous experience. The empath did not come here to be a doormat or a dumping ground for the rest of humanity. It is the responsibility of the empath to show others where healing may occur and to bring out the best in them. It is impossible for the empath to reach these goals and fulfill this purpose if they themselves are subject to constant overwhelming situations.

Rest is imperative to the health of all people, but especially for the empath. It is in rest time that the empath can recharge and return to self. Sleep is sometimes like a reset button for the empath, and in the sleeping state, they can work through and dispose of the energy that does not belong to them. Therefore, the empath will feel much better after a good sleep.

We need to be kind to ourselves and rely on our own inner judgment and perception. We cannot do that if we have no love for ourselves. While it is difficult for the empath to love themselves, it is one of the most important things they can do. If you do not love yourself, how can you ever propose to love anything outside of yourself? It is not the responsibility of the empath to act as a container for the problems of the world. It takes great strength to stand up for yourself and to say no to all that which does not serve you positively. The willpower that it takes the first time that you do this is immense. However, the more you do it, the better you will feel and the more natural it will come to you.

Chapter 9: Tools and Suggestions for the Empath

This chapter could be an entire book on its own. However, I have placed here the most important advice that I could give to other empaths for them to find more happiness and stability in their lives. This advice could probably be given to anyone. However, as it is in the empath's nature to get overwhelmed with the sheer amount of information out there, I feel it is important to narrow it down for the beginner so that there is a place to start. As with everything, remember that this book is advice and wisdom learned through my own life and through my research, so only take the advice that resonates with your life. There is no information in this world that is worth taking on if it does not sit well with your soul. And that is probably the most important advice. Never agree to anything that does not feel right. Listen to your gut, always.

Meditation, Awareness, and Being Present

There is so much literature on the positive aspects of meditation and mindfulness that it is difficult not to have heard these words before. Meditation does not mean thoughtlessness or at least without thought. It means spending time alone, or in a group setting, in a state of quiet reflection and deep introspection. There are many forms of meditation, and there are still more variants of these forms.

It is not uncommon for someone to find great healing through the practices of meditation and mindfulness and then become a teacher in this field. Once becoming a teacher, it is then, not uncommon for a person to add their own flavor to the practice. Therefore, we have so many branches of meditation practices. At its core, meditation is nothing more than being aware of what is going on inside the self. You can meditate on a specific thought, area of the body, situation in life, and the list goes on. Meditation does not need fancy tools. All meditation requires of you is to find a place where you will be undisturbed and be able to quiet the mind. When you try to focus and unrelated thoughts get in the way, don't try to fight them, instead acknowledge the thoughts, place them in an imaginary bubble, and allow them to float away.

Meditation requires practice, and a dedicated practice at that. Meditation practiced early in the morning will be far more productive than meditation practiced at the end of the day. It is difficult to focus and exercise the willpower needed for lengthy periods of sitting still when you are tired. Guided meditations are also fantastic for practicing visualization and finding information about the self in a short amount of time. There are many different meditation teachers who provide excellent guided meditations to assist you in your journey. I suggest that you browse through YouTube to find a meditation that you are drawn to so that you can see what works for you. Some people like guided meditation or specific sounds and instruments. Find what works for you.

Mindfulness and being present in the moment are another imperative addition to the empath's toolbox. Sometimes the mind is too busy and overthinks everything. When we are mindful of our present moment, there is less chance of us living in the future or the past. It is important to be grateful for this moment right here and not live with regret, or in a constant perception of what ifs? Mindfulness of the present moment sounds easy enough—it is not. To help you on your path to becoming more mindful, and more aware in this moment, try to place triggers around your home. Triggers can be anything from pictures to sticky notes with messages like "how do you feel right now?" or something like an alarm, which is not too loud, that reminds you to be aware of your surroundings.

Holding Supportive Space

One of the little truths in life is that you can take the horse to the water, but you cannot make it drink. This applies to all people. Every person holds within themselves the answers they need to navigate this world. You cannot save anyone; they can only do that for themselves. If a person does not want help, there is nothing you can do that will change their mind. It is not the responsibility of the empath to make up their minds of the surrounding people.

It is the responsibility of the empath to understand how to hold supportive space when it is needed. The empath must learn about the subtle art of nonverbal communication, and how to allow a person to speak their truth and find their own answers. This requires a deep understanding of how to listen and not just hear what other people are saying. The problem with this is that the empath already knows what the other person is feeling or thinking, and therefore understands, perhaps even before the conversation began, what the solution looks like. It helps absolutely nothing to tell someone else what they ought to do with their life. With many personalities, this will only push them in the opposite direction of healing.

To hold supportive space, the empath must learn to lighten the load effectively by sharing in the experience and by allowing the other person to speak their hearts out. By truly listening to understand and not just listening to simply reply, the empath will master the art of indirectly healing others. Holding supportive space is truly an art, and requires a great deal of patience, love, empathy, and deep understanding. These are qualities that naturally exist within the empath. If the empath can learn to truly listen patiently, they will be an important asset in facilitating healing in the world around them.

The Empath in the Workplace

There are a lot of opinions about how the empath truly operates in the workspace. As we discussed earlier in the book, not everything is written in stone. While it depends greatly on the skill set of the empath in question, in addition to their specific personality type beyond the Myers-Briggs, the empath generally does better when they work one-on-one with other people.

The following lists of career options that work and do not work are generalizations. There are too many variables to consider to provide you with a blueprint of what works and what doesn't. Nonetheless, let us dive into the generally accepted list of positive and negative career options for empaths.

Careers that Work

- Therapist
- Graphic Designer
- Artist
- Librarian
- Musician
- Counselor
- Social Worker
- Veterinarian
- Life Coach
- Psychologist
- Religious Leader
- Self-Employed

Careers That Do Not Seem to Work

- Salesperson
- Cashier
- Politician
- Managers
- Journalist
- Butcher

Something very interesting about empaths is that they have a tough time to remain in a career or job that does not serve the greater good. If they are working in an area where they believe they are of no help to humanity, they will not stay in it for a long time. Empaths thrive in environments that are harmonious, authentic, and useful. Empaths do not care for the race toward money and power and therefore, any job relating to marketing in a company that they do not believe in is the worst decision that they can make. The empath needs to feel needed and at the same time as though they are benefiting the rest of the world by doing what they're doing. Writers and artists are almost always the hidden empaths who satisfy their desire to help the rest of the world through artifactual and other forms of nonverbal communication. You may believe that there are hard and fast rules to give empaths boundaries, but there really are not. These are the generalizations. Remember, just because you are an empath does not mean that you have not already successfully adapted to cope better than others.

Conclusion

Is the empath real? Yes. The empath is a true warrior in this digital age. I do believe that the empath has a great responsibility to usher in a new world concept of compassion, authenticity, and divine understanding. There are so many people who need love and just someone to listen, and there is no one better to do this than the empath. The life of the empath is rich with experience, and this is perhaps so for them to understand far more than the average person.

Perhaps I'm wrong not to refer to the empath as a superhero, and perhaps that is the empath in me that refuses to acknowledge this pedestal. I know that some mornings without my first cup of coffee, I definitely do not feel like a superhero. Humor aside, I have come to understand that empaths the world over are the gentle heart of Mother Earth; they are the innocence and the hope that can transform this planet into the beauty that it has the potential to be.

I urge every empath to remember that prioritizing self-care is highly important, not selfish. There is no use in trying to heal the world if we cannot first heal ourselves. This book is so close to my heart, and it is my desire that it will be a guiding light in the life of empaths and those who have an empath in their life. Every word has been carefully organized to represent a holistic picture of the experience that empaths endure. There is a lot of controversy, because there are many types of empaths, and the world also seeks petri dish results that our species cannot yet produce.

Until we are able to prove the existence of the empath beyond a shadow of doubt, it will be difficult to explain the exact nature of this human enigma. The truth is, we exist. And while empaths should take care to work in careers that are conducive to their mental, physical, and spiritual well-being, many do not have this luxury. Empaths are found everywhere in the world, and some are fighting it out in soul-destroying environments, thinking they've lost their mind and wishing they were like the rest of the world.

My message to every empath in the world is that I salute you for your bravery, your perseverance, and simply because you are here at this time on this planet to bring hope back to humanity. The gentle nature of the core aspects of the empath is not to be mocked and ridiculed. But to be celebrated because they are the reason for greater compassion, and perhaps the real answer behind solving some of the world's greatest problems. If empaths could rule the world, we would have no wars, there would be no famine, and humanity would be awarded the nurturing, compassionate sense of community that it deserves.

I hope that all the information in this book will bring you, my reader, great peace and understanding about empaths. I also hope that if you are an empath, that you will take the time when you put this book down to go look in the mirror and tell yourself how grateful you are for this life and how very needed you are. Never forget your inner compass, because it is the sole intuition, this heartfelt understanding that knows the purpose that you are to fulfill in this life. And if you respect your inner being, it will never steer you wrong. Remember who you are and listen to the whispers of personal truth on this path. You are the master of your own life and regardless of social norms, you should understand that everything you are is absolutely perfect for the purpose which you came to fulfill on this planet.

Acknowledgments

I would like to express heartfelt love and thanks to my friends and family for supporting me through the manifestation and fruition of this book. I would also love to give back that support and love by listing their small business websites where applicable. Please support and nurture the success of others!

Thank you to my soulmate husband Paul, who found me again in this lifetime, grows with me, and believes in me day after day. I love you.

Thank you to my mom Tena and dad Harold for giving me the spiritual guidance and space while growing up to come into my own beliefs about God and spirit, and for encouraging me to find my own relationship with God.

To my mom for always allowing me, without judgment, to experience life on my own terms, no matter the consequence.

Thank you to my big sister and big supporter Jeanine, who, even though she's far away, makes me laugh and calls me often but never calls me "crazy." You're far away but never far from my heart. https://JeanineCollins.po.sh

Thank you to my soul family Emma, who also found me again in this lifetime, kicked my spiritual awakening into high gear, and continues to inspire me every day with their talents. https://www.embermischief.com/

Thank you to Source God, my inner being, and my spirit guides for helping me to learn and grow spiritually while in this vessel; and a special thanks to Josie and Burritt for allowing me to borrow their names.

Thank you to my first book review launch team ever – the most patient group of supporters – whose excitement for my success is inspiring:

Steve Piscitello, Emily Danault, Shane Flynn, Nakia Johnson, Tiffani Hull, Adam Bennett, Laura Waller, Katie Williams, Monica Johnson, Grace Lyons, Diane Gilbert, Jeanine Collins, Sarah Petrin https://www.sarahsemporiumunique.com/, and others who simply did not want the credit by name.

And finally, to my two children, Alessandra and Axel, who may read this when they get older as they come into their own beliefs… Follow your inner voice and your heart always. Care about how you feel. It is *everything*. My love for you is eternal and unconditional. I love you, "no matter what."

About the Author

Josie "May" Barrett is an Intuitive Spiritual Awakening Guide. She's also an author, certified (accredited) meditation teacher, reiki master, small business owner, empath, and most importantly, wife and homeschooling-stay-at-home Mommy to Alessandra and Axel. Josie gained expertise and psychic mediumship abilities while having her own spiritual awakening. These skills allow her to personally and intuitively guide people who are having their own spiritual awakening. Josie lives in Massachusetts with her family.

Website: https://josiebarrett.com/

Email: jb@josiebarrett.com

Facebook Page: https://www.facebook.com/josiebarrettauthor

Instagram: https://www.instagram.com/josiebarrettauthor/

References

Abraham-Hicks Publications. (2021, August 17). *About Abraham Hicks.*
Retrieved August 17, 2021, from https://www.abraham-hicks.com/about/

American Psychiatric Association. (n.d.). *What Is Somatic Symptom Disorder?* Retrieved July 18, 2021, from https://www.psychiatry.org/patients-families/somatic-symptom-disorder/what-is-somatic-symptom-disorder

American Psychological Association. (2019, December 4). *The Decline of Empathy and the Rise in Narcissism with Sara Konrath, PhD* [Video]. YouTube. https://www.youtube.com/watch?v=UaZeDKwnvg8&t=2s

Armstrong, K. (2017, December 29). *'I Feel Your Pain': The Neuroscience of Empathy.* Association for Psychological Science - APS. https://www.psychologicalscience.org/observer/neuroscience-empathy

Blagrove, M., Hale, S., Lockheart, J., Carr, M., Jones, A., & Valli, K. (2019). Testing the Empathy Theory of Dreaming: The Relationships Between Dream Sharing and Trait and State Empathy. *Frontiers in Psychology, 10.* https://doi.org/10.3389/fpsyg.2019.01351

Buck, A. (2021, March 26). *What Is It Like to Be an Empath? True Stories and Real Life Experiences.* LetterPile. https://letterpile.com/serializations/What-Is-It-Like-To-Be-An-Empath-True-Stories-and-Real-Life-Experiences-Part-2

Cambridge Dictionary. (2021a, July 21). *compassion definition: 1. a strong feeling of sympathy and sadness for the suffering or bad luck of others and a wish to. . .. Learn more.* https://dictionary.cambridge.org/dictionary/english/compassion

Cambridge Dictionary. (2021b, July 21). *creativity definition: 1. the ability to produce or use original and unusual ideas: 2. the ability to produce or use. . .. Learn more.* https://dictionary.cambridge.org/dictionary/english/creativity

Center for Academic Research & Training in Anthropogeny. (n.d.). *Empathy | Center for Academic Research and Training in Anthropogeny (CARTA).* Retrieved June 14, 2021, from https://carta.anthropogeny.org/moca/topics/empathy

Decety, J. (2010). The Neurodevelopment of Empathy in Humans. *Developmental Neuroscience, 32*(4), 257–267. https://doi.org/10.1159/000317771

Dispenza, J. (n.d.). *Stories of Transformation.* Unlimited with Dr Joe Dispenza. Retrieved July 30, 2021, from https://drjoedispenza.com/pages/stories-of-transformation

Dr Joe Dispenza (2020) - HOW TO CURE BLINDNESS by Dr Joe Dispenza Meditation (Nurse Healed). (2020, April 22). [Video]. YouTube. https://www.youtube.com/watch?v=4S_HzMsTJ3Y

Goldberg, A., & Scharf, M. (2020). How do highly sensitive persons parent their adolescent children? The role of sensory processing sensitivity in parenting practices. *Journal of Social and Personal Relationships, 37*(6), 1825–1842. https://doi.org/10.1177/0265407520911101

Heym, N., Kibowski, F., Bloxsom, C. A., Blanchard, A., Harper, A., Wallace, L., Firth, J., & Sumich, A. (2021). The Dark

Empath: Characterising dark traits in the presence of empathy. *Personality and Individual Differences, 169,* 110172. https://doi.org/10.1016/j.paid.2020.110172

Inge, C. H. (2020, October 15). *Empath vs Empathy: What is the difference?* Christie Inge. https://christieinge.com/empath-vs-empathy/

Inside Science. (2018, March 30). *Telepathy Is Real | Inside Science.* https://www.insidescience.org/video/telepathy-real

ISSUP -. (2017, July 14). *Emotional Contagion: Everything You Need to Know.* International Society of Substance Use Professionals. https://www.issup.net/knowledge-share/resources/2019-11/emotional-contagion-everything-you-need-know

James, P. F. [Frank James]. (2018, June 12). *Myers-Briggs 101: What are the Cognitive Functions? || MBTI 101* [Video]. YouTube. https://www.youtube.com/watch?v=fUOkMm43hGM

Lancey, D. F. (2021). *The Anthropology of Learning in Childhood (2010–01-16).* AltaMira Press.

Lingnau, A., Gesierich, B., & Caramazza, A. (2009). Asymmetric fMRI adaptation reveals no evidence for mirror neurons in humans. *Proceedings of the National Academy of Sciences, 106*(24), 9925–9930. https://doi.org/10.1073/pnas.0902262106

MedicineNet. (2020, December 16). *Do Hypochondriacs Feel Real Symptoms?* https://www.medicinenet.com/do_hypochondriacs_feel_real_symptoms/article.htm

Montag, C., Gallinat, J., & Heinz, A. (2008). Theodor Lipps and the Concept of Empathy: 1851–1914. *American Journal of Psychiatry, 165*(10), 1261. https://doi.org/10.1176/appi.ajp.2008.07081283

Myles, A. (2017, November 2). *Why Empaths could be Wrongly Diagnosed as Bipolar. | elephant journal.* Elephant Journal | Daily Blog, Videos, e-Newsletter & Magazine on Yoga + Organics + Green Living + Non-New Agey Spirituality + Ecofashion + Conscious Consumerism=it's about the Mindful Life. https://www.elephantjournal.com/2017/10/why-empaths-could-be-wrongly-diagnosed-as-bipolar/

Myss, C. (2015, August 17). *Appendix: A Gallery of Archetypes.* Caroline Myss. https://www.myss.com/free-resources/sacred-contracts-and-your-archetypes/appendix-a-gallery-of-archtypes/

News Medical. (2019, February 27). *What are Mirror Neurons?* News-Medical.Net. https://www.news-medical.net/health/What-are-Mirror-Neurons.aspx

The One-Way Speed of Light | Spaceaustralia. (2021, January 27). Space Australia. https://spaceaustralia.com/news/one-way-speed-light

Pallipedia. (n.d.). *What is Empathy - Meaning and definition - Pallipedia.* Retrieved July 27, 2021, from https://pallipedia.org/empathy/

Psycom.net. (2021, May 18). *Narcissistic Personality Disorder (NPD): Causes, Symptoms, Treatment.* Psycom.Net - Mental Health Treatment Resource Since 1996. https://www.psycom.net/personality-disorders/narcissistic/

Raine, A., & Chen, F. R. (2017). The Cognitive, Affective, and Somatic Empathy Scales (CASES) for Children. *Journal of Clinical Child & Adolescent Psychology, 47*(1), 24–37. https://doi.org/10.1080/15374416.2017.1295383

Riess, H. (2017). The Science of Empathy. *Journal of Patient Experience*, *4*(2), 74–77. https://doi.org/10.1177/2374373517699267

Rizzolatti, & Sinigaglia. (2015). Curious Book on Mirror Neurons and Their Myth. *The American Journal of Psychology*, *128*(4), 527. https://doi.org/10.5406/amerjpsyc.128.4.0527

Ruhl, C. (2020, August 7). *False-Belief Task: Sally Anne*. Simply Psychology. https://www.simplypsychology.org/theory-of-mind.html

SciShow Psych. (2019, June 17). *What Do Mirror Neurons Really Do?* [Video]. YouTube. https://www.youtube.com/watch?v=pGYKcqzG_7M

Scott, J. C. (2012). *The Darker Side of Life* [E-book]. GoodReads.

Serious Science. (2016, December 30). *Theory of Mind - Uta Frith* [Video]. YouTube. https://www.youtube.com/watch?v=N6ylH-LYjOM&t=651s

Siegel, E. (2021, January 26). *The Dream Of String Theory Is An Unlikely Broken Box*. Forbes. https://www.forbes.com/sites/startswithabang/2021/01/26/the-dream-of-string-theory-is-an-unlikely-broken-box/?sh=68ae26cb3b3f

Smithsonian Institute. (n.d.). *Genetics | The Smithsonian Institution's Human Origins Program*. Retrieved July 23, 2021, from https://humanorigins.si.edu/evidence/genetics

Stapleton, P., Dispenza, J., McGill, S., Sabot, D., Peach, M., & Raynor, D. (2020). Large effects of brief meditation intervention on EEG spectra in meditation novices.

IBRO Reports, 9, 290–301. https://doi.org/10.1016/j.ibror.2020.10.006

The Myers Briggs Company. (n.d.). *The history of the MBTI ® assessment*. Retrieved July 23, 2021, from https://eu.themyersbriggs.com/en/tools/MBTI/Myers-Briggs-history

The Secret. (2020, May 16). *History of The Secret | The Secret - Official Website*. The Official Website of The Secret. https://www.thesecret.tv/history-of-the-secret/

Theosophy Downunder. (2008). *Theosophy Downunder: Newsletter*. http://theosophydownunder.org/ifensterl.php?australiantsewsletterdecember2008.html

Times of Israel. (2018, December 21). *Neuroscientist says her belief in precognition is more than just a hunch | The*. https://www.timesofisrael.com/neuroscientist-says-her-belief-in-precognition-is-more-than-just-a-hunch/

Unlimited with Dr Joe Dispenza. (n.d.). *Scientific Research*. Retrieved July 26, 2021, from https://drjoedispenza.com/pages/scientific-research

USA Today. (2020, August 14). *"The Secret" author Rhonda Byrne's "Greatest Secret" out in November*. https://eu.usatoday.com/story/entertainment/books/2020/08/14/the-secret-author-rhonda-byrnes-greatest-secret-out-november/3374285001/

World Health Organization. (1997, March 13). *WHOs agenda for Electromagnetic Fields research*. https://www.who.int/publications/i/item/WHO-EHG-98-13

Image References

Ayrton, A. (2021, January 11). *Distressed woman in hood sitting in autumn park* [Photograph]. Pexels. https://www.pexels.com/photo/distressed-woman-in-hood-sitting-in-autumn-park-6551497/

Barros, R. (2018, September 10). *Close-Up Photo of Person Behind Leaves* [Photograph]. Pexels. https://www.pexels.com/photo/close-up-photo-of-person-behind-leaves-1692821/

Cottonbro, C. (2020a, February 20). *Photo of a Woman Sitting Beside Statue* [Photograph]. Pexels. https://www.pexels.com/photo/photo-of-a-woman-sitting-beside-statue-3778550/

Cottonbro, C. (2020b, August 20). *Man in White Long Sleeves Holding Dog's Face* [Photograph]. Pexels. https://www.pexels.com/photo/man-in-white-long-sleeves-holding-dog-s-face-5961946/

Filipe, J. (2017, January 16). *Space Story* [Art]. Unsplash. https://unsplash.com/photos/QwoNAhbmLLo

Lach, R. (2012, April 12). *Woman in White Dress Sitting on White Ice* [Photograph]. Pexels. https://www.pexels.com/photo/cold-iceberg-melting-snow-8262600/

Lightpainting, M. (2021, April 12). *Woman With Blue Hair and Red Lipstick* [Photograph]. Pexels. https://www.pexels.com/photo/light-fashion-person-people-7492173/

Piero, L. (2017, February 2). *Man Looking Up* [Photograph]. Pexels. https://www.pexels.com/photo/man-looking-up-312491/

R.F. Studio. (2020, February 23). *Woman Practicing Yoga* [Photograph]. Pexels. https://www.pexels.com/photo/woman-practicing-yoga-3820364/

Rodnae Productions. (2020, December 26). *Light fashion man love* [Photograph]. Pexels. https://www.pexels.com/photo/light-fashion-man-love-6670262/

Sadasivuni, V. (2019, October 31). *Depressed young man with blurred head in dark room* [Photograph]. Pexels. https://www.pexels.com/photo/depressed-young-man-with-blurred-head-in-dark-room-3833370/

Sayles, B. (2019, December 18). *Photo Of Woman Wearing White Shirt* [Photograph]. Pexels. https://www.pexels.com/photo/photo-of-woman-wearing-white-shirt-3406020/

Shimazaki, S. (2020, November 4). *Black woman in pain on sofa* [Photograph]. Pexels. https://www.pexels.com/photo/black-woman-in-pain-on-sofa-5938368/

Shuraeva, A. (2020a, September 12). *Woman in White Crew Neck T-shirt Wearing Black and Silver Necklace* [Photograph]. Pexels. https://www.pexels.com/photo/woman-in-white-crew-neck-t-shirt-wearing-black-and-silver-necklace-6014743/

Shuraeva, A. (2020b, September 12). *Woman in White Lace Shirt Lying on Bed Beside Woman in White Shirt* [Photograph]. Pexels. https://www.pexels.com/photo/woman-in-white-lace-shirt-lying-on-bed-beside-woman-in-white-shirt-6015089/

Shvets Production. (2021, March 31). *Close-Up Shot of an Elderly Woman in Pink Long Sleeves Holding a Jewelry* [Photograph]. Pexels. https://www.pexels.com/photo/close-up-shot-of-an-elderly-woman-in-pink-long-sleeves-holding-a-jewelry-7545400/

Thegiansepillo, T. (2020, February 8). *Woman With Brown Eyes and Black Mascara* [Photograph]. Pexels. https://www.pexels.com/photo/woman-with-brown-eyes-and-black-mascara-3808991/

Valerio, K. (2016, January 4). *Man Wearing Black Cap With Eyes Closed Under Cloudy Sky* [Photograph]. Pexels. https://www.pexels.com/photo/man-wearing-black-cap-with-eyes-closed-under-cloudy-sky-810775/

Verrecchia, F. (2017, January 17). *Standing Woman Facing a Speeding Train* [Photograph]. Pexels. https://www.pexels.com/photo/standing-woman-facing-a-speeding-train-298018/

Voguel, M. (2018, November 11). *Dreamy young woman touching mirror in autumn forest* [Photograph]. Pexels. https://www.pexels.com/photo/dreamy-young-woman-touching-mirror-in-autumn-forest-7239462/

Made in the USA
Las Vegas, NV
01 May 2025